T0132469

Life's
a Classroom

Ten Powerful Lessons for
Living Your Best Life

Nani Solares, MS

BALBOA.
PRESS

A DIVISION OF HAY HOUSE.

Balboa Press books may be ordered through booksellers or by contacting:

Balboa Press
A Division of Hay House
1663 Liberty Drive
Bloomington, IN 47403
www.balboapress.com
1 (877) 407-4847

Print information available on the last page.

ISBN: 978-1-5043-6883-4 (sc)
ISBN: 978-1-5043-6885-8 (hc)
ISBN: 978-1-5043-6884-1 (e)

Library of Congress Control Number: 2016918027

Balboa Press rev. date: 11/15/2016

"The first time I met Nani was on a missionary trip we took together to Thailand in 2012. One thing that immediately stood out to me about Nani was that she was able to see things in people that I couldn't even see myself. I have known her now for over 4 years and have come to learn that she is amazingly gifted at being able to understand what people are going through. In addition, she has a tremendous heart for helping hurting people. The wisdom that she has gained through her personal experiences, as well as her ministerial and educational background, allow her to bring clarity and outside-the-box solutions to life's many problems. Her faith also allows her to see God's possibilities in the midst of seemingly impossible situations.

When I read *Life's A Classroom,* I couldn't help but get excited about what I was reading. As I read through the manuscript, the words flew off the pages bringing clarity to some things I had been dealing with in my personal life. My family and I were experiencing some challenging circumstances at the time, but after reading Chapter 2, it was settled for me. Nani's wisdom and amazing way of explaining key points will enable anyone to grow in life. This book is a gold mine to anyone who values wisdom, wants to change and wants to continue progressing in life. I am blessed to own the treasure of *Life's a Classroom.* I can assure anyone reading this book that it is an investment that will exponentially add value to your life."

-Pete Cabrera, Jr.

This book is dedicated to God. To some, that may seem strange, but there is no One more real to me than Him. How He got me from the mess of the person I was to who I am today, I will never know. Nevertheless, here I am, sharing what He has given me with the world, seeing lives changed every day. Thank you so much, my Father, Savior, and Best Friend. Truly, You encompass everything I need in this life. May every day of my life, from here until the end, be lived with purpose, in service to You and others.

In loving memory of my precious grandmother, Nana, one of the best students of life that I have known. Nana, you learned to live well despite many reasons not to. Your legacy of love will live on in the lives and hearts of all those who knew you. Indeed, to know you was to love you and to be loved by you.

November 27, 1923–August 2, 2016

Contents

Introduction

Hi there. Thank you so much for your interest in reading my little book. I have to say, I have thoroughly enjoyed writing it. It has truly been a labor of love.

I initially decided to write this book after various people encouraged me to put my life's wisdom in book form. It made a lot of sense to me, so I decided to take the plunge. After all, it is my passion to share what I have learned along the way. Indeed, through the course of the last fourteen years of my life with God, I have learned lessons that were not only life-changing but utterly invaluable. As I wrote about the lessons that are now a part of my heart and soul, it excited me so much to realize how powerful they could be for you as well. It is for this reason that I have packed all the love that I could possibly muster into each and every word.

As a psychotherapist, minister, and inspirational speaker, I often tell people that I am not just the president; I am also a client. That is a reference dating back many years to a commercial for a hair restoration company for men. In a brilliant effort to cause future clients to identify with him, the president of the company admitted that he too had been a patient of hair restoration surgery. This phrase stuck with me after all these years because I too see myself as someone that hurting people can identify with. Indeed, of all the lessons I have learned, most have been wrought through the overcoming of my own pain and struggles, i.e. the classroom of life—hence the name of this book.

Don't get me wrong: I do have many degrees, trainings, and certifications that go along with what I do for a living. I have sat in many an academic classroom and learned all about theories and psychotherapeutic approaches and modalities. And they have served me well inasmuch as they have provided foundational principles for my counseling practice. But the practical wisdom that allows me to navigate life in a healthy, successful, and happy way was developed through my own journey of change, healing, and personal growth.

In February 2002, I hit an emotional rock bottom. I use the word *emotional* because, physically speaking, my life was virtually intact. I had not lost my job, my home, or my family. But I felt emotionally bankrupt and was laden with emotional pain that I just could not suppress any longer. It was in my darkest hour on that February day that I collapsed, both literally and symbolically. I *literally* collapsed because I fell on the floor of my apartment and sobbed like I was dying. I experienced such hopelessness in that moment that I did not know if I would ever recover. It was also *symbolic* because the physical collapse represented the inward collapse of the façade that seemingly held it all together. I have always referred to that day as the day of "my nervous breakdown." Except that instead of calling 9-1-1, I called Jesus Christ.

After crying out to Jesus, He literally showed up, and from that moment on my entire life changed. I was suddenly full of hope for my future and determined to change my life. And for the last fourteen and a half years, that is exactly what I have been doing. I have been actively pursuing God the Father, His son Jesus, and His precious Holy Spirit. I have been learning to love and accept myself radically and unconditionally—concepts I knew nothing of prior to 2002. I have had the opportunity to experience amazing things that have led to great insights and spiritual awakenings. I have learned to transcend my past and the things that happened to me. I have learned powerful, profound, and practical wisdom that has made my life easier and way more enjoyable.

Learning from life is exactly what this book is all about. It delves into all of these aspects to some degree. But the main purpose of *Life's a Classroom* is to provide readers with practical wisdom that will allow them to live their best lives. I have learned life is what we make of it and happiness is a choice. I have learned that it is not what happens to us, but how we react and respond to what happens to us that makes life easier or harder. Life is life at the end of the day, but few people realize the impact and power they possess within themselves to create either the life of their dreams or their nightmares.

Since I started this journey, my greatest desire has been to help people transform their lives, just as mine was transformed. I love that I now get to be part of the journey of those who have honored me with their trust. It is a gift to pay it forward and witness as individuals who choose to learn from life change and recreate their lives. Furthermore, I am so thankful to God for giving me the opportunity to live my dreams and work in my passion.

The process has brought me to the realization that there was a plan for my life from the very beginning. In fact, I learned that God had been working in my life years before that fateful day in 2002. My heart had actually begun to look for answers to my problems a few years back. All too often, though, I stumbled around in the dark, unable to find my way. Little did I know, that was all God needed in order to begin to unravel the greatness of His plan for me.

In January 2002, I made the life-changing decision to change my career. It was a bold move considering the security I had as an administrator for my family's business. Nevertheless, I went back to school to study psychology and obtained a Master of Science degree in 2005. Flash forward approximately ten years later: I am now a Licensed Mental Health Counselor with the state of Florida and own my own counseling agency, which I lovingly called *Nani's Place.*

Nani's Place was the manifestation of a dream that I had in my heart for many years. Currently, it is still a new business and is in the process of morphing into what I have long envisioned. The dreams and visions I have for my life are extremely big, thus I know Nani's Place is only the beginning. It is the first stepping stone in fulfilling my desire to bring God's redemptive power and love to the many hurting in South Florida and the world over.

Though only in retrospect, I can now see that the last ten years of my profession have been a step-by-step preparation for future endeavors. I have been fortunate enough to have the richest of experiences and training opportunities during my years in the mental health and social services industry. The exposure that I have received throughout my career has given me a firsthand look into the needs of the hurting in our world, as well as insight as to how to intervene.

Years of working with hurting individuals, not to mention going through my own healing journey, have enabled me to acquire firsthand knowledge of human behavior and what it takes to change. I have studied in-depth the role that the mind and the brain play in creating our lives—something that has taken a foundational role in what I do.

Whether I am working with a child, an adult, a couple, or a family unit, my approach is threefold: 1) I work to uncover self-defeating thought patterns and behaviors, often at the unconscious level; 2) I work to empower individuals to make life-affirming choices by calling out the God-given, innate gifts and abilities within each person; and 3) I offer a safe environment of love, compassion, understanding, and support, enabling individuals to open up to the process of change. I have found this approach to be extremely effective and much briefer than traditional approaches, which too often keep people bound to their past.

At Nani's Place, our motto is, "Restoring families and communities, one person at a time." And every day, we are doing just that. This book is yet another extension of that deep desire to see lives restored. What's more is that all of the principles delineated in this book are the same ones we work to instill in our clients, so they too can live the lives they want.

Though I may not be able to work with each reader individually, I have written this book to help you glean from what I have learned—often the hard way. Given that this is my first book, I felt it important to provide information that will enable you to understand where I am coming from. This is precisely why I decided to share my heart and my background in this introduction.

As a student of life myself, I am only drawn to speakers who clearly walk out what they preach. As far as I am concerned, the messenger is equally as important as the message. Thus, I have vowed to first learn and then teach. And, believe me, I haven't arrived yet. Not by a long shot! I am totally okay with that, though, since I have learned that life is truly lived in the journey, not the destination. As a good pupil, my job is to remain humble and teachable, as this is the approach most conducive to learning. Indeed, it is when we think we know it all that we become most ignorant.

In fact, life is so eager to teach us when we become willing to learn that the lessons are endless. For this reason, the challenge in writing this book was not a lack of content—quite the opposite actually. Indeed, the harder part was determining what that content *should* be. Thus, I decided to narrow it down to my top ten life lessons.

In addition, the reader should not be surprised to find that many themes are repeated throughout the book. This is because many of these topics overlap with one another. This only serves to prove the importance of these lessons and how oftentimes one depends upon the other. The good student will also note that repetition is always part of the learning process. And as we will see, life is all too happy to repeat lessons until they are fully grasped.

Life is beautiful, yet it can be awful depending on our attitudes, belief systems, and choices. The wisdom in these ten chapters has allowed me to make the most out of life. These lessons are practical things that, when applied, have powerful results. Most important, as you read this book and begin to adopt the lessons in it, you too will begin to adjust your mindsets and belief systems, causing permanent changes in your mind and brain. This is the greatest key when it comes to change and creating the life you want. What's more is that within these ten lessons you will begin to realize what an important part of the plan *you* are. Consequently, you will awaken to the inherent power and potential that God has deposited within you.

Moreover, it is my hope that after reading this book, you will never again see yourself as a helpless victim of life, but as an overcomer and a victor. I pray you will realize that you are someone who can succeed and thrive in this life. And my greatest desire for you, dear reader, is that as you read this book, you too will become an avid student of life.

As you read, be encouraged in the knowledge that the lessons in it are for you as much as they are for me. No one is special in that we are *all* special. What God has for one, He has for all. So make sure to personalize it as you go through it. In addition, I pray that you will find this book encouraging, refreshing, and uplifting, as my heart's desire is to always bring out the best in people. May you enjoy the reading as much as I have enjoyed the writing. Lastly, thank you for giving me the opportunity to be a part of your journey, however small.

Until we meet again (or until my next book), happy trails, fellow traveler ... Happy trails ...

Lesson 1

Life's a Classroom

L ife truly began for me at age twenty-seven. That is when I had the nervous breakdown that changed my life forever. At that time, I was struggling with depression, addictions, self-hate, and a world of emotional problems. And on February 20, 2002, a.k.a. "nervous breakdown day," everything reached fever pitch. That turned out to be both the worst and best day of my life. Finding myself in a terribly desperate and hopeless place, I did the only thing that made sense: I prayed for death.

In that moment, I could not fathom taking another step toward my life. The thought of getting up the next day, going to work, and doing it all over again seemed impossible from that vantage point. As I lay on my living room floor in the fetal position, I was suddenly reminded of something I had heard the pastor say the week before at church: "When you feel you need help, call out to Jesus, and He will help you." Having no other recourse, that is exactly what I did.

Much to my surprise, like a knight in shining armor, He actually showed up. I could feel His presence in my living room as His supernatural peace filled the place. Though I did not understand what was happening at the time, I knew it was real. Lying there, unable to move, I was suddenly struck by the realization that everything was going to be all right. Indeed, it was a much-welcomed change from the hopelessness of the prior moment. Somehow I also knew that nothing was ever going to be the same again. And, by golly, it wasn't.

That was the day I embarked on a healing journey that would leave no stone unturned. Though volumes could be written about the journey itself, it is beyond the scope of this book. Instead, I will be sharing with the reader the most powerful lessons I have learned under the tutelage of life. The title of the book itself actually conveys the first and most pivotal lesson about life—*it is a classroom, and we are here to learn.*

A classroom is only as great as its teacher. The classroom of life also has a great teacher. His name is God. God is the focal point of life, and every lesson points right back to Him. The following verse from the Amplified Bible beautifully accentuates this point:

> She will bear a Son, and you shall call His name Jesus [the Greek form of the Hebrew Joshua, which means Savior], for He will save His people from their sins [that is, prevent them from failing and missing *the true end and scope of life, which is God*]. (Matthew 1:21 AMP)

God is the true end and scope of life. Our main purpose is to live in and share intimacy with Him. This truth has been reflected back to me in each and every life lesson. For me, life is God, and God is life. The two cannot be separated. They are one and the same. He gave me life, sustains my life, and gives my life purpose. Thus, I have learned that anything gleaned apart from Him is deception.

The fact is that we are here to learn, and God is eager to teach us. To that, one might ask, "What exactly are we here to learn?" The answer is, *anything and everything*. There is so much *to* learn. Every circumstance and event in our life offers deep lessons concerning life itself, God, the world, relationships, even ourselves. And every day provides new opportunities and a new lesson plan, whether we participate in it or not.

While life can certainly be challenging at times, I have learned the fundamental truth that it is *for* me and not *against* me. To live is to continuously grow in God. It is a journey, not a destination. If we did not learn, we would not grow. We would remain stunted in our spiritual and emotional maturity. Growing and learning makes life easier as we go along. Indeed, we are meant to be emotionally and spiritually evolving at all times. To *evolve* means: "To change or develop slowly, often into a better more complex, or more advanced state: to develop by a process of evolution" (Merriam-Webster's Online Dictionary, n.d.).

I find an interesting contrast between physical evolution and emotional and spiritual evolution. It is not by choice that our bodily functions are in constant flux, i.e. our body is aging, our organs are performing their respective functions, and our cells are continuously dying and reproducing. These are processes of the human body that happen automatically and organically. While physical evolution takes place automatically, it is not so with its emotional and spiritual counterparts. Nay, emotional and spiritual evolution and growth occur *by choice*.

I am reminded of a sad, yet profound, moment in my life when someone I knew passed away. As I stared at his lifeless body in the coffin, I had the realization that though he lived a relatively long life, he failed to learn from life what is truly important. I found myself doing what I hope no one ever does at my funeral—praying to God that I would never be like him. Although he had amassed substantial financial wealth and was acquainted with prominent members of society, his family relationships were in disarray. He allowed money to get in the way of love. His legacy of anger and division is still alive and well in those he left behind. In my estimation, he lived and died and never got a clue. As a result, he robbed himself of life's true riches.

I don't know about you, but I want to leave a legacy for my children, grandchildren, and future generations of love, destiny, and a life lived with purpose. And today is the day that we can make that happen. But we can only do so by choosing to be good students of life.

The classroom setting is made up of all sorts of students: good ones, mediocre ones, bad ones, and everything in between. There are students who love to learn. They feel enriched by the acquisition and application of new information. To this type of student, learning's ups and downs and mistakes and failures challenge them to grow and meet the obstacles ahead with gusto. On the other hand, there are other students for whom learning and school are drudgeries. They dislike being challenged by new information. Learning's ups and downs and mistakes and failures are seen as stressful and unpleasant.

Academically speaking, I was never a good student. I did not have good study habits growing up, and school was primarily a means of social interaction and tomfoolery. I always managed to get average grades, but learning was definitely not my priority. What's more, years of struggling and procrastinating caused me to develop some negative attitudes about learning. This caused me to struggle all the more in college. Thus, my legacy of mediocrity lived on. After getting my Associate in Arts degree, I dropped out and vowed to stay as far away as possible from higher education. I told myself it was not for me and passively accepted my fate.

Then, years later, there was a glimmer of hope, a pivotal life-changing moment when I dared to dream that my life could be different. In January of 2002, I went back to school to study psychology, and for the first time, things *were* different. This time, I was there because I wanted to be. In addition, there was a real personal investment inasmuch as I was paying my own tuition. I was thoroughly interested in what I was learning. I was excited about my classes. And something funny happened: I got straight A's.

As my attitude and self-confidence level changed, I was amazed to discover some hidden qualities I did not know I possessed: *intelligence and determination.* They were there all along but had been hidden for years beneath negative perceptions about myself, as well as the learning process. When those perceptions started to change, so did my performance.

The classroom of life is very similar. Our attitude about learning will determine what we learn and how far we go. If we want to learn what life—and by extension, God—has to teach us, then it will behoove us to become good students. Being a good student of life begins with making the conscious decision to learn. Without that, many lessons will slip right by us. A good attitude about learning is also important to avoid the risk of developing mindsets that stunt our growth and sabotage our happiness.

Conversely, negativity is toxic to life. When we hold negative attitudes toward life, we fail to learn what it is trying to teach us and subsequently create negative outcomes. We become our own worst enemy. It is also important to note that being a good student, academically speaking, does not necessarily make a good student of life. Indeed, intellectual people often run the risk of trying to figure everything out with their heads, whereas most of life's lessons require a combination of our heads and our hearts.

In addition, the good student will quickly realize that life is full of choices. And God loves us enough to allow us to make those choices. Free will is the result of the freedom found in God's unconditional love. Moreover, free will choices, made day by day, create our destinies. Indeed, life is always trying to teach us the value and power of our choices. It is in these lessons that we learn to be successful and fulfill our dreams and goals. On the other hand, it is in our refusal to cooperate with life that we struggle needlessly and experience dysfunction.

Like the not-so-good student, we too can have negativistic attitudes that hinder learning and growth. Some of these include, but are not limited to, having a victim mentality, self-pity, entitlement, laziness, and apathy. The attitude behind these mindsets is often bitterness or resentment toward life. Therefore, people with these mindsets tend to view the experiences common to life as negative and unfair. Though they may not realize it, this becomes a vicious cycle in that it creates more negative attitudes, which in turn create even more negative outcomes.

Truly, life is a mixed bag of a myriad of experiences: joy and pain, blessings and loss, happiness and sadness, disappointment and excitement, and so on. Sometimes Christians get the wrong idea about what it means to be a follower of Jesus. They develop a belief that being a Christian means an absence of problems. But Jesus did not offer us an absence of problems; He offered us assurance of victory over anything that life may bring.

> I have told you these things, so that in Me you may have [perfect] peace. In the world you have tribulation *and* distress *and* suffering, but be courageous [be confident, be undaunted, be filled with joy]; I have overcome the world. [*My*

conquest is accomplished, My victory abiding.]. (John
16:33 AMP)

I believe that an absence of problems would not be beneficial for
us, as it would stunt our spiritual and emotional growth. We learn
through both positive and negative experiences. It is unhealthy to
live with the expectation that everything is always going to go our
way because that is just not reality.

Indeed, I have met people who have all but scripted their lives
out like playwrights. They have fixed concepts of what their lives
should look like, and they get frustrated when things do not fit the
script. Interestingly enough, most of the people I have met who are
happy and fulfilled will say that life did not turn out at all as they
had envisioned. But because they were flexible and open to the
changes and lessons wrought into every day, it turned out better
than they could have imagined.

This has definitely been my experience. I too had a script for
my life. However, looking back, I realize that the plans I had in
my mind were quite superficial. They certainly did not incorporate
the twists and turns of life and the role my own spiritual evolution
would play in it. Today I feel that plan would have left me feeling
extremely empty. Truly, I have found God's plan, although vastly
different than what I expected, to be richer and more fulfilling than
I could have dreamed possible.

One day, while praying and meditating, I had an experience
with God that brought this point home in a very real way. In my
quiet time, I felt led by the Holy Spirit to visualize the canvas of my
life, i.e. the life I had created for myself thus far. He revealed to me
that in many ways, I was resisting His plan—not because I did not
want His plan, per se, but because I had my own ideas about what
my life should look like. Then, driving the point home further still,

He told me to envision myself taking white paint and a paintbrush and painting over the canvas until it was completely blank. Next He said, "Now put down the paintbrush. I'll take it from here."

Learning of God's unending love for me has enabled me to believe, with every fiber of my being, that He has a good plan for my life. I also learned that my plan apart from Him did not work out—though not for lack of trying. So when He asked me to put down the brush and allow Him to do the painting, I was more than happy to do so. Seeing God's plan unfold through my cooperation has enabled me to have a good attitude toward life and learning. From this perspective, any problem I may have is automatically framed through the light of His love and goodness. Through it all, I have put one foot in front of the other in trust, knowing that He works it all out for my good. And something crazy keeps happening—one way or the other, it always does.

Charles Swindoll said that life is 10 percent what happens to us and 90 percent how we react to what happens to us. What if we started responding to every circumstance, whether negative or positive, from the perspective of, "What can I learn from this?" When we learn to ask ourselves what life might be trying to teach us through each experience, we will find that our attitudes toward negative circumstances will change for the better.

Moreover, when we realize that life is not against us but for us, we naturally take on a more hopeful and positive attitude. Positive attitudes, in turn, create positive outcomes in our lives. Therefore, by taking this approach toward life, we will become our own best friends and greatest allies in creating destiny.

Additionally, those powerful attitudes and mindsets will open doors to success and breakthroughs. Our heart will open even more to learning, and as a result, we will learn all the more. The more we learn, the more we grow and evolve. As we strengthen our spiritual muscles, we learn to get out of our own way, and life becomes easier to manage. Over time, we find true happiness. We are no longer dreading negative experiences as we find they are fewer and further between. When we do have problems, past learning and positive attitudes allow us to confront things head on, thereby allowing us to move from problem to solution in no time.

At the end of the day, we are the common denominator. It is our attitudes, mindsets, and belief systems that determine the choices we will make in life. Furthermore, it is our choices that determine our outcomes. Things that seem unfair happen to us all. Thus, a powerful principle I have learned is that of personal accountability. Indeed, we all have problems at times, but add to those problems a bad attitude and poor choices, and now we *really* have problems.

As for anyone with a "woe is me" attitude toward life, my advice it to lose it fast. It serves absolutely no productive purpose but only creates worse problems and impairs our ability to learn from life. An inability to learn will not only keep us stuck in our problems, but it will wreak an endless cycle of chaos and dysfunction in our lives.

Along that same vein, here is another funny little fact in regard to learning from life: To learn is a choice, but if we refuse to learn, we will always get *reruns*. Life will attempt to teach us, whether we want to learn or not. And if we fail to learn the lesson, it will attempt to teach it to us again, and again, and again.

Rerun is a term used for television programs that are airing again after the original air date. We are on a pass/fail system with life. In other words, when we pass, we move on to bigger and better lessons. The opposite is also true. When we refuse to learn, we continue to get reruns of our past problems. As a result, life gets harder and harder. Every time we let a lesson slip by, we lose the opportunity to learn powerful coping and life skills necessary for living well. Our emotional and spiritual growth becomes stunted, and, by consequence of that, we end up having undue emotional pain. I am thankful that I got the memo about reruns early on and heeded it. Here is what it said: *Learn lessons, have less pain; fail to learn lessons, have more pain.* I opted for the former. I hope you will too.

The bottom line of this entire chapter is this: whether we choose to learn or not, life's a classroom. Therefore, make life easier on yourself and choose to be one of God's best students. Like any good parent, God is most concerned about our growth and development. It pleases Him greatly when we have a student's attitude toward life because He knows that will allow us to experience His best. The more we learn, the more we manifest what we were created to be and reflect His nature and glory. Today, choose to be a good student. Learn the lessons your life is teaching you. Have a good attitude toward life experiences and, most important, enjoy the learning.

Lesson 1: Life's a Classroom
Questions for Self-reflection

1. I mentioned in this chapter that in the classroom of life there are good students, mediocre students, and bad students. In what ways have you been a good student of life? In what ways have you been a not-so-good student?

_____

_____

_____

_____

2. What attitudes do you possess that have helped you learn from life?

_____

_____

_____

_____

3. What attitudes have impaired your ability to learn from life?

_____

_____

_____

4. Whether you categorized yourself as a good, mediocre or bad student of life, how can you become an even better student of life?

_____

_____

_____

_____

5. Will the awareness of reruns help you approach life circumstances in a different way? How so?

_____

_____

_____

_____

Lesson 2

The Lesson within the Lesson

Life is teaching us all sorts of valuable and amazing things. What we may not realize, though, is that there is a lesson within every other lesson that life is teaching us. That lesson is, "Will you trust God?"

We are here from God and for God. The purpose of life is relationship *with* God. Relationship with God is similar to relationship with other people, but in many ways, it also differs. God is not only our God. He is our Father. He is our Savior. He is our Helper. He is our Provider. He is our *everything*. Unaware though people may be to this fact, God is our Source for life. From the beginning, we were created to live out of relationship, union, and dependence upon Him. But man lost sight of that for a moment, and as a result, separation from God ensued.

When I read about creation in the book of Genesis, I am captivated by the beautiful love story of the relationship between God and man. The Bible says that God created mankind in His image and likeness. In the Garden of Eden, God created the world and everything in it even before he created Adam and Eve. Thus, it is clear to me that the earth was created *for* man. It was God's gift *to* man. And dominion of it was also given over to man. Everything mankind needed was already provided. People did not have to go out and get anything for themselves but lived in the plenitude of the kingdom at their disposal. It was not until the fall that mankind had to go out and work to survive.

Enter Jesus Christ. It is often emphasized that the purpose of the cross was to take away our sins. Although this is indeed accurate, it is only scratching the surface of the true power behind the cross. In fact, the main purpose and crowning achievement of Jesus's death and resurrection was the reconciliation of relationship between God and Man—and by extension, the restoration of the union we once enjoyed with God. Because humans were never created to live separate from God, after the fall, we intrinsically began malfunctioning and self-destructing. We were suddenly fending for ourselves and living independently, which was never God's plan. Jesus spoke of this as recorded by John in his Gospel:

> I AM the True Vine, and My Father is the Vinedresser. Any branch in Me that does not bear fruit [that stops bearing] He cuts away (trims off, takes away); and He cleanses and repeatedly prunes every branch that continues to bear fruit, to make it bear more and richer and more excellent fruit … Dwell in Me, and I will dwell in you. [Live in Me, and I will live in you.] *Just as no branch can bear fruit of itself without abiding in (being vitally united to) the vine, neither can you bear fruit unless you abide in Me.* I am the Vine; you are the branches. Whoever lives in Me and I in him bears much (abundant) fruit. *However, apart from Me [cut off from vital union with Me] you can do nothing.* If a person does not dwell in Me, he is thrown out like a [broken-off] branch, and withers; such branches are gathered up and thrown into the fire, and they are burned. If

you live in Me [abide vitally united to Me] and My words remain in you and continue to live in your hearts, ask whatever you will, and it shall be done for you. (John 15:1–2, 4–7 15:1–2, 4 AMP Bible)

I believe these verses speak more of dependence upon God than of salvation itself. A person can be saved and never learn to live dependent on God. Indeed, we can be saved for thirty years and still live a dysfunctional life in what the *Alcoholics Anonymous* book calls, "self will run riot" (2001). Self will run riot represents a life lived following our base instincts and trying to fulfill our own plans and desires apart from God's. It speaks to me of the baby Christian who never learned that he is no longer living to and for himself but living to and for God (2 Corinthians 5:15 NKJV). And it wreaks havoc upon our lives, because when we live according to our base instincts, we inevitably end up out of balance and in trouble.

Jesus Himself is the source of life. He is the vine; we are the branches. A branch is connected to the vine. The source of life runs through the vine and into the branch. The fact that the branch is plugged into the vine is what allows life to constantly flow into it. When we live a life dependent on the life source of Jesus Christ and the presence of the Holy Spirit living in us, His life source flows into everything that we are. *This is true dependence.*

This is exactly the point that Jesus was emphasizing in the story of the Samaritan woman at the well: "But whoever takes a drink of the water that I will give him shall never, no never, be thirsty any more. But the water that I will give him shall become a spring of water welling up (flowing, bubbling) [continually] *within him* unto (into, for) eternal life" (John 4:14 AMP)

This infamous story of God's grace starts off with Jesus meeting the woman at the well, where she was getting water, something that would have been a daily chore for her. Jesus was not there by accident. He knew in His heart that this was a very thirsty woman. He gets the emptiness and pain of her soul and offers her something that sounds crazy to the natural ear—*living water,* water that will permanently quench her thirst. Clearly, Jesus is not talking about H2O here. He is speaking directly to the angst and pain of her soul. And what He is offering her is nothing less than His very life living within her.

The Samaritan was a woman looking for love in all the wrong places. But Jesus knew there was only one love that could satisfy her every need. *Water,* from a spiritual sense, represents salvation, cleansing, and the presence of the Holy Spirit. In the new birth, we are offered the same thing Jesus offered the woman at the well: *those who believe in and therefore rely on Him will find a river (or source) of living water (divine life and divine resources) on the inside of them for every need* (John 4:14 NKJV). Indeed, receiving Jesus as savior is a package deal. That package includes salvation, the presence of God, and the fullness of the kingdom and its resources—*all living on the inside of us!*

Along with the invitation to receive the package deal made available by His Son, God is offering us a life of dependence and reliance upon Him and His resources. Some people believe this represents blind obedience to God, like a soldier taking orders without questioning why. Others think that dependence means having to ask God at every turn what His will is. But this is not dependence; it is immaturity.

The best model of true dependence upon God was Jesus Himself. Furthermore, His life exemplified the epitome of spiritual maturity. Jesus was a busy guy, yet He often needed quiet time with His Father for the refreshment of His soul. Anyone who spends any significant amount of time in ministry and helping people knows this is a must to avoid burnout. Jesus was not exempt from this need, which is why a common theme in his teachings was His union with the Father.

Readers and students of scripture would be wise, though, not to interpret this as blind obedience. The flaw in this logic falls in the idea that believers are mere servants of God. The New Testament, and Jesus Himself, make it abundantly clear that we are sons, not servants: "*No longer do I call you servants*, for a servant does not know what his master is doing; *but I have called you friends*, for all things that I heard from My Father I have made known to you" (John 15:15 NKJV).

At the end of the day, what good is blind obedience if we do not truly trust our master? Paul, writing to the Galatians, reiterates this point from the New Covenant perspective: "And because you are sons, God has sent forth the Spirit of His Son into your hearts, crying out, 'Abba, Father!' Therefore *you are no longer a slave but a son, and if a son, then an heir of God through Christ*" (Galatians 4:6–8 NKJV).

True New Covenant dependence is born out of knowing our identity and flowing in our authority as sons and daughters of God and heirs to His kingdom. When was the last time you saw an heir of an earthly kingdom struggling to obtain or begging for anything? Similarly, as heirs to the kingdom that created riches and has the ultimate authority, we have no need to beg for anything. Jesus did not beg. He took what He needed and got whatever He wanted. Neither did He stop and ask His Father what He should do around every corner, because a son instinctively knows what to do. The reason a son knows what to do is because a true son possesses the heart of the Father and deeply understands His will.

Understanding His identity, Jesus only needed to exercise the authority of the kingdom to fulfill the will of God from moment to moment, as needed. The will of God is quite simple. It is to do good and meet the needs of the hurting by enforcing the victory that Jesus won at the cross. And there is never a need to ask God if we should do that. As New Covenant children of God, everything we do flows from intimacy, or relationship, with God. Thus, anything outside of relationship is simply dead religion.

Indeed, true dependence flows from relationship. From this perspective, dependence upon God is as simple as sharing our lives and hearts with Him, partnering with Him, and relying on His resources. It means knowing that we can trust Him with everything—our entire lives, even. This may sound like a very difficult thing, but when we know God from a place of intimacy and have become acquainted with His character, it is not hard at all. It is quite easy, actually.

Hebrews 11:11 is a powerful scripture that illustrates the simplicity of true faith: "Because of faith also Sarah herself received physical power to conceive a child, even when she was long past the age for it, *because she considered [God] Who had given her the promise to be reliable and trustworthy and true to His word*" (AMP).

Sarah was able to conceive after she entered menopause because she trusted in the nature of God. She knew Him intimately and had come to understand His faithfulness at a deep level. She had experienced it time and time again through relationship. Sarah knew she would conceive, not because God was powerful necessarily, but because she was acquainted with his character. Past experience had taught her that if God said He would do something, it was as good as done. *Because she knew Him well, she trusted Him infinitely.*

Every day offers new opportunities to turn to God in trust. Every experience and situation begs the question, *"Will you trust God?"* And every circumstance, positive or negative, great or small, is an opportunity to learn of God's goodness and faithfulness. Life itself constantly beckons us to stand still so we can see the glory of God (Exodus 14:13 NKJV).

When the proverbial poop hits the fan, we stop, breathe, and then simply have a conversation with Our Creator and Papa. We learn to yield in the moment before taking matters into our own hands. We invite Him into the situation, asking Him for wisdom, waiting on Him for a solution. In the meantime, we enjoy our day. Fear and worry stem from an absence of trust. Learning to truly trust God allows us to rest and enjoy our lives, knowing that things are in good hands with the Almighty.

Like most people, I struggled with wanting to control my life. I feared uncertainty until I realized I had no choice. Uncertainty is simply a part of life. It is not something to be feared but something to be accepted—embraced, even. Acceptance of uncertainty has given me a fresh perspective on not knowing, as well as on the process of change itself.

To trust God is to acknowledge humbly that we do not have all the answers. It is surrendering the need to know everything. It is learning to be led in life instead of going it alone. I finally realized that I was on a *need-to-know* basis with God, and the future is *not* a need-to-know. In humility, I accepted this, and as a result, found great comfort in the fact that He *does* know everything. We are much better off when information is in God's hands anyway because He always knows what to do with it. We, on the other hand, do not always possess that ability. That is precisely why *He* is God.

Before, when I thought about my future, I looked upon it with dread. I shuddered at all of the scary *what-ifs* that possibly awaited me. Today I see the future as an exciting adventure that I get to discover as it evolves one day at a time. Actually, now when I think about my life and future, a beautiful mental picture is conjured up in my mind. In it, I see myself as a little girl dancing with my heavenly Daddy. We are doing that thing that little girls just love to do. I am riding on His feet as He leads me in a riveting dance. I can see myself laughing and having a grand old time as He leads my life to new and exciting places. I have no idea where we are going, but I am thoroughly enjoying going along for the ride. In the dance of life, I can let Him lead because I have learned that wherever He is taking me is exactly where I want to go.

People have this crazy notion that to live is to suffer, to worry, and to fear. As a result, many individuals arc forever bracing themselves for the other shoe to drop, in expectation of the next catastrophe. The world teaches that, not God. God says exactly the opposite. Indeed, life is a beautiful journey to be thoroughly enjoyed. In the good times, we relish everything we are learning and get so much out of our partnership with Him. In the tough times, we hang on to Him like white on rice and stand still until we see His glory in the situation.

Truly, trust and reliance upon God bring deep peace and enjoyment of life because the pressure is off of us. Ultimately, intimacy and dependence are about inviting God into all the details of our lives since He has already invited us into His. Not to mention that, by virtue of creating us, He has made it clear He wants to be a part of everything that has to do with us.

In theory, this sounds amazing to most people. The problem is that the world has trained us to be *self-reliant*. God-reliance will not come naturally until we make it a point to invite Him in. Thus, practicing the presence of God is paramount to learning dependence upon Him. The more we become aware of His constant and abiding presence, the more we will naturally turn to Him when negative things happen. The key is actually not to overcomplicate it, as there is no formula or perfect way to pray. It is as simple as nurturing our relationship with Him and watching it grow. And it is available to every one of us.

So today, take the leap of faith. Learn to be led. Learn to rely on God, and you will find that His resources far outweigh any that you may bring to the table. Know too that God is not drawing you to a life of deep intimacy and reliance to take away from your life, but to add richly to it.

Today God is extending an invitation for you to take a ride on Daddy's feet. Where you will go, only He truly knows. *Only He is meant to know.* Once you are dancing, though, you will quickly find that it was never about the destination anyway, but it has always been about the dance. I submit to you then, dear reader, in the famous words of Lee Ann Womack: "If you get the chance to sit it out or dance ... I hope you dance ..."

Lesson 2: The Lesson within the Lesson
Questions for Self-reflection

1. Do you have difficulty sometimes seeing the *lesson within the lesson* (Will you trust God?)?

   _____

   _____

   _____

   _____

2. If so, what do you think causes you to miss it?

   _____

   _____

   _____

   _____

3. What areas of your life would you say have been characterized by self-will run riot, i.e. living according to your base instincts with little to no awareness of the consequences? What have the results of self-will run riot been in your life?

   _____

   _____

   _____

   _____

4. Does your relationship with God reflect more of a partnership of intimacy and oneness or a boss telling his subordinate what to do?

   _____

   _____

   _____

   _____

5. What attitudes or belief systems hinder you from seeing yourself as a partner and cocreator with God in his divine plan?

_____

_____

_____

_____

Lesson 3

Be Yourself; Everyone Else is Already Taken

In early 2002, only two short months into my journey of recovery from alcohol abuse, I attended a spiritual retreat. Anyone who has been through early recovery will understand just how raw I was at the time. Times were truly rough, but God was working overtime to divinely orchestrate all things healing. And this retreat was no exception. Although I received many gifts from those three days, one of the most important moments was hearing a message on the subject of *wearing masks*. It moved me to the core as I realized I had been doing just that for a very long time.

I remember crying for about an hour after that message. Feeling paralyzed, I sat dumbfounded in the chair as I contemplated the effect it had had on me. The blinders had been lifted and, as a result, I suddenly felt so saddened by what I had done to myself for so many years. A lifetime of inferiority and low self-worth had led me to believe that I could not be myself around others. Given the choice, I would have jumped at the opportunity to be anyone other than me.

Wearing masks for so many years prevented me from being my authentic self—something I might have embraced had I any notion as to who *I* actually was. My personality has always been loud and boisterous. Not much has changed in that regard, but prior to the year 2002, I hid a world of pain behind that façade.

I was the party girl. The one who always had a drink in her hand and a fake smile plastered on her face. Though some may have thought of me as the life of the party, I was hiding from myself and everyone else behind that persona. Faithfully, it sheltered me from pain and unconsciously carried me through many storms. And when my fiancée left me for someone else four days prior to our wedding, that façade quickly became survival for me. Terrified of what facing that pain represented, I clung to it as if my life depended on it.

Looking back, I can pinpoint that break-up as the proverbial straw that broke the camel's back. I tried my hardest to keep it together, but after that, things quickly started to unravel. That entire relationship had, in essence, been a lie. I was not truly in love him; he was not truly in love with me. We were merely serving a purpose for each other.

At the time I thought I could only exist in the context of a romantic relationship. Thus, it was a security blanket of sorts for me, the loss of which brought unprecedented pain and shame. Thing is, if you spend your life running, when the poop hits the fan, you quickly find you have no idea what to do with yourself. Such was my situation, making my life a ticking time bomb on the verge of explosion.

So my solution was to do the only thing I knew *to* do: continue hiding behind my masks. I went on as if everything was all right. People often commented on how strong I was and how impressed they were by how I was dealing with everything. Little did they know, I was not dealing with anything *at all*. I was hiding. I was running as fast as I could from myself—and my pain. But everything eventually caught up with me and came to a screeching halt that fateful night in February 2002. All of a sudden, the masks came crashing down, the alcohol no longer worked, and I found myself in a deep and hopeless depression.

Like many people who hide behind masks, I wore masks out of fear—fear that people would not like what they found if they got to know the *real* me. And as if that fear was not bad enough, there was a greater fear that paralyzed me to the bone: *What if in my quest to find myself, I come up empty? What if the search only confirms that there is nothing good in me whatsoever?* The idea of that reality was too much to fathom, so I hid all the more.

Change came one day at a twelve-step meeting when I experienced a cathartic moment. Though I do not recall exactly what was being said that day, I clearly remember the breakthrough. For as long as I could remember, I was a people-pleaser. My identity was based on other people's validation and approval. This is always the case with people who lack self-identity. After all, where do you look for *self*-approval when you have no notion of *self* to begin with?

As a result, I was hypersensitive to and lived in fear of rejection. I often found myself bending into a pretzel to conform to whatever I thought other people wanted, especially when it came to the opposite sex. Interactions with men were never about what I wanted or needed but about what I thought they did. When I thought I figured that out, the contortionist in me came out, fitting myself into whatever mold I thought necessary. Of course, this never actually worked out in my favor since others can intuitively sense when we are trying too hard. Instead of drawing people toward me, oftentimes I ended up pushing them away.

Then I had the catharsis that changed everything. In that meeting, I was suddenly confronted with the futility of my quest to find approval in others. I realized that because I did not approve of and accept myself, no matter how hard I searched for it in others, it would always be insufficient. It suddenly dawned on me that what I was really looking for all along was not the approval of others but myself.

This awakening led me to conclude that in reality there are only two opinions that matter in this world: *God's and mine.* By that time, I had grown enough in God to know that He unconditionally loved and approved of me. So that meant that the final stamp of approval would have to come from none other than me. Truly, all I ever wanted to know was that who I was, was inherently okay. The problem was that I always went about trying to obtain that information in the wrong way. In fact, it had never been up to others to determine that; it had always been up to me. And although God had already given me His divine stamp of approval, it was useless to me unless I agreed.

That day I decided to agree with Him and to have the courage to be myself. As a result, the direction of my quest drastically changed. I stopped the contortionist act and decided that whether anyone else approved of me, I was going to approve of myself. I decided in that moment that I *was* inherently okay. I was more than okay, actually. I was great! With that revelation came an absolute intolerance for phoniness—not so much in others but in myself. Indeed, it hurt too much to sell myself short as I had done for so many years. As I became aware of that, I began to appreciate everything that made me *uniquely me.*

The truth is that every one of God's creations is a unique expression of God Himself. This is obvious to me now when I consider the miracle of human life and the vast differences among us. Creation itself tells this story around every corner.

Consider the miracle of the human fingerprint. Billions of people have passed through this earth, and billions more will pass through it after we are gone, yet no two fingerprints are—or ever will be—alike. Though forensic science has greatly capitalized on this fact, God intended it as a clear message: *Each and every one of us is unique, special, and completely different from everyone else.* Hence the title of this chapter: *Be Yourself; Everyone Else Is Already Taken.*

This is a liberating reality for a world obsessed with comparing one thing to another. All day, every day, we are barraged with comparisons. Ads compare one product to another to determine their worth. Accountants and economists compare the current year to the prior one to determine its productivity. Even now in the United States, we find ourselves in a period of time known for its emphasis on cruel and public human comparisons—a presidential election. But the most damaging of all caparisons is when we turn them toward ourselves, judging ourselves based on the characteristics of others.

The fact that comparisons clearly cannot be escaped in modern reality begs the question: *Are comparisons even accurate?* I personally believe they are not. The fact that there are so many variables at work makes an attempt at an accurate assessment categorically unfair. It sure does not stop us from trying, though.

Things are usually a combination of pros and cons, positives and negatives. Where one product may be lower in price, one may be higher in quality. Therefore, consumers will be drawn to one product over the other based on individual preferences and needs. While product comparisons can definitely be unfair, they pale in contrast to the catastrophic effects of human comparisons. Indeed, there is nothing more unfair and unrealistic than the attempt to compare one person to another.

This is a book about life lessons. And one of the most profound for me was when I learned that each individual is a unique package—God's package. That package includes our gender; our culture; the family we were born into; our experiences, both negative and positive; our personality characteristics; and our distinct gifts and talents. *We are not a coincidence.* There is nothing haphazard about human life because God is not a haphazard kind of guy. He is strategic and specific, and everything He does has purpose. Paul, using Kind David's life as an example, made this point when preaching at Antioch in Psidia:

> "For David, *after he had served God's will and purpose and counsel in his own generation,* fell asleep [in death] and was buried among his forefathers, and he did see corruption and undergo putrefaction and dissolution [of the grave]." (Acts 13:36 AMP)

As we can see by these verses, even the generation we are born into is not coincidental. Everything about who we are is part of a wonderful tapestry created by God. And everything He created is good. Indeed, every aspect of who we are comes together to make each of us completely different from *everyone* else.

Arriving at this awe-inspiring conclusion can undoubtedly be life-changing. It will also inevitably lead us to a decision: What will we do with this information? Will we embrace who God made us to be and be our authentic selves? Or will we ignore it and continue to live a dishonest life? Will we love and appreciate ourselves exactly as we are? Or will we continue to sell ourselves short by trying to be so much like other people?

We are each a masterpiece of God's love and creative power. So when we compare ourselves to others, especially when we come up inferior, not only are we dead wrong, but we damage our self-worth and identity. When I had my realization about wearing masks, it was as painful for me as it was liberating. The pain of suppressing what an infinite God created me to be for the sake of obtaining the approval of others had hurt me to the core. At the same time, by acknowledging and exposing the lie and embracing my authentic self, I was freed to be exactly who I was supposed to be.

Often people tend to see their lives as a race they are running. And more often than not, that race is against other people. This erroneous perspective does more harm than good as it stirs up the desire to compare by putting one person against another. The truth is that we are in fact running a race in life. It's just not against any other person; it is against our *former selves*. The race is against our former selves because if we are to continue to learn and evolve as individuals, then there must be something to compare our progress to. Thus, the only fair comparison is how we are doing now, as opposed to how we were doing in the past.

The only constant is change, and if we are not moving forward, we will eventually start moving backward. However, to compare ourselves to others is just plain dumb. It is the equivalent of attempting to compare my printer to my office chair. They are both necessary but serve completely different purposes. The chair was not created to do what the printer does, and vice versa. In reality, there is only one comparison that can be accurately drawn: Are they performing their function in an acceptable manner according to their purpose? In other words, is the chair being a good chair? Is the printer being a good printer? The same question can be asked about ourselves. Are we functioning the way we were created to function? Or are we malfunctioning by trying to be someone other than who we are?

Nature seems to get it. Inanimate objects even reflect it. But human beings cannot stop competing. As a result, they are constantly opening themselves up to jealousy, rivalry, and a world of ugliness. The human race desperately needs this revelation. People need to know they are perfect just as they are. We were all created to shine in our own way. The problem arises, however, when we try to do it the way others do.

Take Celine Dion, for example. God has gifted her with the voice of an angel. I love to listen to her sing, but for me to attempt to sing like she does would be an exercise in futility. I could practice for fifteen hours a day and get voice lessons from the best coach on the planet, but because I do not possess her talent, it will never happen. Indeed, singing professionally is one aspect of Celine's package, but it is not at all a part of mine. I could spend my time being jealous of Celine and frustrated with myself, continuing to waste precious time and energy trying to be something I am not. Or I could use my time and energy toward developing the strengths inherent in me—the things I do have the potential to excel at. Now that is time much better spent, wouldn't you say?

Jealousy is comparisons on steroids. In actuality, jealousy rarely has anything to do with the other person. Metaphorically speaking, when we experience feelings of jealousy, we are looking in a mirror. When we look in a mirror, the reflection looking back at us is always our own. Frustration over areas of our lives where we know we are not meeting our potential will often elicit feelings of jealousy toward others' achievements. Similarly, when we see other people boldly shining their light in this world, we may become jealous because we know in our hearts that we could be shining ours, but aren't.

On the other hand, when we love and accept who we are and work toward developing what God has given us, we have no reason at all to be jealous. Instead we feel proud of others and experience feelings of admiration toward them. Indeed, every single person has the potential to succeed in this life. For many, success in life is climbing the ladders of financial and career ambition. As for myself, I believe true success is evolving as an individual and developing the gifts and qualities specific to me. It is learning to be my authentic self in the world, shining my light, and loving everything that makes me, me.

People love authenticity. It is indeed a breath of fresh air in a world of clones. While it is great to have mentors and people who model qualities we aspire to emulate, we should not strive to be *just like* our mentors. Truly, when we attempt to do things and shine our light the way others do, we come across as inauthentic. And since people can usually sense inauthenticity, at the end of the day, we fool no one but ourselves. The opposite is also true. People are drawn to authenticity in others. There is something about people who are unapologetically themselves that makes others want to be around them.

When I finally learned to be my authentic self in relationships, I was liberated from the pressure to please others. As a result, I became a magnet for amazing people and experiences. Life became so much more fulfilling as new and amazing doors of opportunity started to open to me. I learned that I could shine in this world in my own unique capacity—and so could others. I was happy for myself—and I was happy for others too. The truth is that the world would be very boring if we were all alike. Thus, when we allow ourselves to be who God created us to be, we do the world a great service by making it balanced and well-rounded.

Some people will love us for who we are. Others will not. Some may even hate us. Who cares? I learned that other people's opinions of me are none of my business. But when we allow our authentic selves to shine through, the people we do attract to our lives will love us for who we truly are. So often, I find people bending over backward to get people to love them. What is the point of that? Do we really want people in our lives who do not have true feelings toward us? As for me, I don't spend much time worrying about those who don't love me. Instead, I go find those who do. It really is that simple.

Another gift of authenticity is the ability to find your *voice*. Your voice represents your truth. It represents your ability to express what is in your heart and to share the message of your life with the world. We all have one. And the world needs to hear it. For some, it may be a cause that is close to their heart. For others, it is learning to stand up for themselves. For others, it is in their newfound ability to say no and set boundaries and expectations in relationships. All of this is part of being true to ourselves because suppressing what is in our hearts when we have something to say is exactly the opposite.

There is a line out of Williams Shakespeare's Hamlet that aptly conveys this message:

> This above all: to thine own self be true,
> And it must follow, as the night the day,
> Thou canst not then be false to any man
> (trans. 1992, 1.3.564–156).

When we are true to ourselves, we are automatically true and honest with others. Authenticity is honesty. It is integrity. By being authentic, we are living honestly, and by being honest, we are living authentically. Overall, we sleep better at night and have a richer life when we love ourselves enough to *be* ourselves. What a great gift indeed we give to others and ourselves when we live our authentic lives. And what a great gift we give to God, who takes such great pleasure in the expression of each uniquely special life.

So today, be yourself. Everyone else is already taken. Love yourself. Embrace everything that makes you, *you*. Love every gift.

Embrace every quirk. Enjoy every idiosyncrasy of your personality. Nothing about you is a coincidence. The wonder of who you are is a gift the world just cannot do without. Courageously set sail on the journey of authenticity. Put your true self forward and trust God and life to bring those who are truly meant to stand beside you. Shine your light boldly. And as you do, you will find support and encouragement from those on the journey who are bravely shining theirs.

Lesson 3: Be Yourself; Everyone Else is Already Taken
Questions for Self-reflection

1. What masks have you been wearing? Why have you felt the need to wear masks?

_____

_____

_____

_____

2. Are you someone that generally approves of and accepts yourself? Or do you often find yourself beating yourself up with judgment or self-condemnation?

_____

_____

_____

_____

3. What specific gifts, talents, and abilities do you possess?

_____

_____

_____

_____

4. How can your unique package make a difference in this world?

_____

_____

_____

_____

5. Have you found your voice yet? What is the message of your life for this world?

_____

_____

_____

_____

Lesson 4

Love to Love Yourself

*L*ow self-esteem. Sadly too many people are familiar with this term. Indeed, it is probably one of the most often-used terms within the self-help arena. Thousands of books have been written on the subject, yet it is still a serious epidemic in our society. It is sad that so many people struggle with their self-worth. Worse yet, it is extremely destructive, as we will see in this chapter.

Technically, I do not use the term *self-esteem* because, from a biblical standpoint, I find it to be a misnomer. I prefer to use the term *self-worth*. Though, in all honesty, I find both terms to be misleading. The term *self* is clearly expressing something in relationship to oneself. Furthermore, the terms *esteem* and *worth* represent *value*. So the compound words *self-esteem* or *self-worth* represent the value one places on oneself. This is precisely the issue I take up with these terms, as they both give the false impression that our worth is up to any of us to determine.

Here is where my view of *self-worth* gets very simple: I am a created being. That means that I was created by a being higher than myself. Had I created myself, it would have been up to me to ascribe a measure of value and worth to my person. But since I did not create myself, it is simply not my right to do so.

To illustrate this point, I would like to provide you with an example: Let's say I am a brilliant computer programmer. And in the pinnacle of my creative genius, I built a computer that far exceeded everything else on the market. Because I am the creator of the computer, I know exactly what went into building it. I know how much memory it has. I am aware of its speed. I am intricately aware of what it can do. And I know all too well its potential. Therefore, I am the *one* person who can state accurately how much the computer is worth.

An interesting thing happens, though, as I present my amazing gift to the world—an entire peanut gallery of critics rises up to contest the value that I placed on it. It seems that everyone has something to say on the matter. However, the true value of the computer is not up for debate. The peanut gallery may not agree with it, but as the creator of the computer, I have the right to sell it at whatever cost I want—even if no one buys it. Thus, the peanut gallery's perspective as to the value of my computer, at the end of the day, is completely irrelevant.

You are probably already starting to get where I am coming from here. I do not care how many people have risen up in your lifetime as the peanut gallery to contest your worth and value. I do not even care how many years you, yourself, have believed that you are worthless, dumb, ugly, or a failure. The truth is that while the peanut gallery clearly does not get a say in determining your worth, neither do you. Why? *Because you did not create yourself.* God, the Great Creator and the Mack Daddy of all computer programmers, is the only one that gets a say. And here is the beauty of it: He has already spoken on the matter, and it is not up for debate.

There is a common problem that I find among Christians. These are the so-called people of God who read the Bible and proclaim it from the mountaintops. Yet sometimes they refuse to believe what

God says. He says one thing; they say another. And the worst part is that many are oblivious to it. They go through their lives without ever questioning core beliefs and thought patterns, many of which pertain to the way they view themselves. Most people think that the epitome of pride is thinking too highly of oneself. I, on the other hand, do not agree with that statement. For me, contradicting God—or *arguing with God*, as I like to call it—is the epitome of pride.

Now, most people will agree that it is outrageous to contradict God, yet it is exactly what many do with regards to self-worth. When we hold negative and erroneous perspectives about our worth, we are, in essence, arguing with God. Self-esteem is a misnomer because *the self cannot determine its own worth. It is up to its Creator to do that.* It really is that simple. So why, then, are so many people walking around with low self-worth, inferiority, and self-hate? The answer to that is also quite simple: They lack an understanding of the intrinsic worth inherent to each one of God's creations.

Given this reality, it stands to reason that when we have feelings of worthlessness, inferiority, or self-hate, we are 100 percent wrong in our perspectives. We are arguing with God because He has spoken on the matter, yet we are choosing to say something different. It is said that it is human to err, so there is no judgment for the wrong perspectives of the past. But for future reference, if we hold a different perspective from God's, it is not God who needs to make the adjustments. It is not He who is wrong. Too many people try to get truth to mold itself to their philosophies, but it is our philosophies that have to yield to truth. And this particular truth is not only a life-changer—it is also a lifesaver.

The worth that God, by His grace, deposited into each and every one of us is intricately woven into every book and chapter of the Bible. It is evident in the story of creation, when God did not think it too much to make us in His very own image and likeness. It is evident in the fall of man and the immediate implementation of God's plan for redemption. It is evident in the love of the blameless Messiah, who gave up everything to dwell among us. It is evident in the Passion of Jesus Christ, a series of events that forever changed history, our nature, and our relationship with God.

The word of God is not only a picture of Jesus Christ and God's redemptive plan for the world; it is a picture of an intense love that would stop at nothing to be in the presence of another. So often we emphasize the seeking of God's presence in Christian circles. But do we ever stop to realize the awe-inspiring fact that God created us because He wanted to be in *our* presence?

Ask yourself this: Why would God create us other than because He wanted to, *because He wanted us?* Did He *really* need warriors that badly? Had things gotten so far out of His hands that He could not handle them anymore? Surely, God did not create humans just for dominion and/or authority. Those aspects, amazing as they may be, are merely part of God's divine purpose for the human race. In reality, we were created because God wanted to spend time with us—*all time.*

When people paint God as having created us for battle, and battle alone, they remove love from the equation. God is love, and everything He does has to be done in love and for love. That includes us. Isn't this is a breath of fresh air to the millions of people walking around the earth feeling unloved and unwanted? Indeed, the world would be radically different if human beings would grasp just how much love and desire went into the creation of every single life. When we think about our lives from this perspective, we quickly realize how wrong we have been about many things. Kind David, in one of His most beautiful and powerful psalms, wrote about a moment when he too was hit with this revelation:

For You did form my inward parts; You did knit me together in my mother's womb. I will confess and praise You for You are fearful and wonderful and for the awful wonder of my birth! Wonderful are Your works, and that my inner self knows right well. My frame was not hidden from You when I was being formed in secret [and] intricately and curiously wrought [as if embroidered with various colors] in the depths of the earth [a region of darkness and mystery]. Your eyes saw my unformed substance, and in Your book all the days [of my life] were written before ever they took shape, when as yet there was none of them. (Psalm 139:13–16 AMP)

This very Psalm was one that God used in my life to set me free from the lie of low self-worth. Truly, when I came to understand self-worth in this way, it was absolutely liberating. The truth came to make me free, but I had to grab hold of that truth to make it mine. And as I did, my erroneous perspectives had no choice but to shift.

Indeed, low self-worth does not exist but in one's erroneous perspectives. Nevertheless, the power of perspective cannot be underestimated. This is because our perspectives and expectations are constantly creating our reality. An eye-opening truth is this: God thinks and believes wonders about who we are, but if we do not agree with Him, we will only create what *we* believe. Thus, it stands to reason that if we want to have the kind of life that God wants for us, we must believe as *He* believes and perceive as *He* perceives.

When we look at self-esteem from this perspective, it seems quite logical and simple. The fact remains, however, that many still struggle to accept the simplicity of it. The reason being is that the world is a humongous peanut gallery that has a lot to say about everything and everyone. In the book of Romans, Paul talked about the power of transformation found in the renewal of the mind. And he emphatically linked life change to our thought life, i.e. perspectives, paradigms, belief systems, etc.

> And do not be conformed to this world [any longer with its superficial values and customs], but be transformed and progressively changed [as you mature spiritually] by the renewing of your mind [focusing on godly values and ethical attitudes] … (Romans 12:2 AMP)

This verse clearly indicates that true mind renewal is changing our perspectives and beliefs to align with God's. Ergo, if we want our lives to change, our thought life must take the lead. On the other hand, low self-esteem and low self-worth are born out of erroneous worldly philosophies dictated by the *zeitgeist*. According to Wikipedia, *zeitgeist* can be defined as "(spirit of the age or spirit of the time) … the dominant set of ideals and beliefs that motivate the actions of the members of a society in a particular period in time" ("Zeitgeist," n.d.).

The zeitgeist is exactly what Paul was referring to in using the term *world* in the above verse. *World* is translated from the Greek word *aion*, which represents the world's ways and ideals. It expresses the notion that society itself decides collectively what is good and what is bad, what is right and what is wrong, what has worth and what does not, what is of value and what is not.

Consequently, it is not hard to fall into the many traps that lead to low self-worth, especially if we do not have an adequate grasp of our true identity. These traps include, but are certainly not limited to, the world's ideals with regards to outer beauty, social status, human potential, success, and acceptance. We are constantly barraged with explicit and implicit messages as to what constitutes worth and what does not. Thus, the automatic response of the natural man is to compare himself to the zeitgeist. And as he does, he hopes and prays that he can somehow measure up.

The problem with this mentality is that the ideals of the world system are created in such a way that no one can measure up. These are inflated, superficial, and irrational ideals that no one person can fulfill. Thus, the search to find our worth and identity in these things only leads to greater emptiness and worthlessness. The world's ideals will cause us to feel superior one moment, only to feel inferior the next. This world is very fickle. Today you are loved; tomorrow you may be hated. Today you are wonderful; tomorrow you may be viewed as a pariah. So, if our self-ascribed value is based on the world's ideals, it will be unstable at best.

On the other hand, the value that God invested in us is innate. It was deposited into every cell of our being. We were born with it full and intact. What's more is that we will leave this world with exactly the same amount of worth that we came into it with. It never rises, nor does it fall. It cannot increase because we cannot possibly possess any more value than God's own value. And it cannot decrease because it is intrinsic to our being. Nothing we accomplish in this world can add to it. And no mistake that we make, no matter how grave, can take away from it.

Our achievements only serve to enrich our lives and fulfill our purpose on the earth. But in the reality of things, they can do nothing to enhance our value. Whether you are Osama bin Laden or Mother Teresa, you have the same worth and value. You can die in this world and never have had a clue as to your true worth, but that still does not change the facts. Truth is truth, whether we believe it or not. And the beauty of it is that we can do nothing to change God's mind about us. He has settled it within Himself—we are all absolutely amazing! Accepting this is the key to knowing our true worth.

To say I used to have low self-esteem is a gross understatement. What I suffered from was more like intense self-hatred. Somehow I got the message that I did not have worth and that I was unlovable. Somehow I got the message that I was inferior. Somehow I got the message that I was a failure. Somehow I got the message that I was ugly and unattractive. Somehow I got the message that I was inherently defective and no one would ever want me. Somehow, from the beginning of my life, there was a peanut gallery that always had something to say about my value and worth. And eventually, that peanut gallery was me.

I am thankful for the therapist I had at the time because she was able to quickly discern my self-worth problem. Through her support and edification, she became a reflection to me of my intrinsic worth. In addition, she was integral in helping me realize the extent of my negativity in thought and word. She corrected me in love every time she heard me speak something derogatory. And as a result, I eventually started correcting myself.

I was also growing every day in my intimate relationship with God, which was helping me to see myself more clearly. I had so many rejection issues when I started, but when I came to know the radical love and acceptance of God, low self-esteem, inferiority, and rejection no longer made any sense. The only thing that made sense to me in the light of His crazy love was to love Him right back and, by extension, to radically love and accept myself.

Before I started my journey with Jesus, I could not have told you more than two or three positive qualities that I possessed. But slowly, as His love unfolded toward me and my perspectives started shifting, I was able to learn so much about myself. I learned I possessed talents and gifts that I had no clue about. I learned I was smart, witty, and kind. I learned I was funny and charming. The more I sought to know God's love, the more I learned about what made me special and unique. *And the greatest thing of all is that I am still learning!*

I found out early on that I was a treasure that needed to be discovered—*by me.* God put the treasure in me, so He knew it was there all along. I just had to become ready to dig it up. Indeed, every single one of us is a treasure chest of amazingness. And God gets unspeakable joy from watching His children uncover the beauty of the treasure within. But we each have to choose to take Him at His word and accept the invitation to find our true selves in Him. When we do, though, it will bring deep satisfaction to our lives. In addition, we will quickly realize it is what we were looking for all along.

Today, know that you too are a treasure that gets to be discovered—*by you.* Ask God to help you become aware of the immeasurable value and worth that you possess. Ask the Holy Spirit to help you see yourself as the Father sees you. It is a powerful prayer with life-changing results.

Today, know that God has called you to love yourself. And not just to love yourself, but to *like* yourself thoroughly. Enjoy spending time with *you.* Enjoy getting to know *you.* You are God's special, unique creation. You are worthy of your own love and acceptance.

Having a revelation of God's love and directing that love toward yourself will, in turn, dramatically affect your relationships with others. You will find yourself having healthier and happier relationships based on pure feelings and honesty. You will no longer require that others carry the heavy burden of constantly having to validate your worth. Once you come to learn it for yourself, it will never be in question again. You will know your worth, and it will be expressed in all aspects of your life and choices, leading you into the abundant life Jesus died for you to have. So today, don't waste any more precious time on self-loathing and self-judgment. Instead, *love to love yourself.* You are worthy!

Lesson 4: Love to Love Yourself
Questions for Self-reflection

1. What has the peanut gallery of the world had to say in the past about your worth and value? How have those messages affected your life?

    _____

    _____

    _____

    _____

2. Low self-esteem, self-hate and self-judgment are examples of "arguing with God." In what ways have you been arguing with God and why?

    _____

    _____

    _____

    _____

3. What damaging messages about yourself have you internalized as a result of the *zeitgeist* -- the world's philosophies and paradigms regarding worth?

    _____

    _____

    _____

    _____

4. Based on God's truth and design for humans, can you now see that your negative self-perceptions have been inaccurate all along? How will this awareness change your life? What part do you play in it?

    _____

    _____

    _____

    _____

5. How will the information in this chapter change the way you view and approach your personal mistakes and failures?

_____

_____

_____

_____

Lesson 5

Own Your Power of Choice

Truth be told, there are millions of people walking around this world in a great deal of pain. And there are myriad reasons as to why they are hurting. While there are certainly many factors beyond our control, I have learned that most of the problems in people's lives are self-created. This is not always a popular viewpoint, though, as many people live their lives in search of a scapegoat to pin their misfortune on. Sadly, this only serves to perpetuate our problems since excuses do not bring change. Only taking responsibility for our choices can bring about the change we desire.

As you may have already surmised, for much of my life I was extremely dysfunctional. I had problems in just about every aspect of life. I had dysfunctional relationships. My self-worth was down the tubes. I was unhappy. I had multiple addictions. I could literally go on and on. The truth is that I saw myself as a victim of life and perceived life as utterly unfair toward me. I believed that just about everyone else had been dealt a better hand than I had. I wondered why everyone got to be happy but me.

Like others in this position, I often played the blame game. You know the one: blame Mom … blame Dad … blame God … blame anyone and everyone—*except myself*. I failed to make the connection between my choices and their ensuing consequences. This lack of insight, in turn, created a vicious cycle in my life that only brought more pain and dysfunction. Thank God that eventually all of it brought me to my knees.

When I started my journey of healing, I was fortunate enough to have people around me who taught me about personal responsibility. Not unlike the rest of the human race, I had experienced many negative life circumstances. But when I had the courage to look at my life honestly, I found that the majority of my issues could be traced back to my own choices.

I was unhappy with my life for many years. But for the first time ever, I realized that the only way things could be different is if I stopped playing the blame game and started looking in the proverbial mirror. I have often heard it said that when you have one finger pointed toward someone else, there are three more pointing back toward yourself. Pointing the finger at the wrongs of others, while temporarily gratifying, is an exercise in futility. Indeed, we cannot fix anyone but ourselves. For this reason, personal responsibility is the only way to create permanent change. This was beyond a doubt the catalyst that started to turn my life in a new direction, and I know it will do the same for you.

In life there are victims and there are overcomers. I have worked with many of each, and there is a vast difference in the trajectory that each of their lives take. Victims choose to blame people for the way their lives turned out. As a result, they remain victims until their viewpoint changes. Overcomers are individuals who despite challenges, pain, and opposition take personal responsibility for their lives, which includes healing from and overcoming the past.

Overcomers refuse to view themselves as victims. The idea of giving the people who hurt them undo power by allowing them to live in their minds through anger, hate, and unforgiveness repels them to the core. By choosing to heal—and forgive—they are able to take their power back and thereby move forward into an unfettered future full of hope.

We have all heard stories of individuals who have been able to forgive unimaginable sins against them. We have also heard of the many people who have turned their pain into a powerful mission for good in the world. Likewise, every day we hear stories of people overcoming seemingly insurmountable obstacles and making their dreams come true. All of these stories are about overcomers. Indeed, it is extremely powerful and courageous to choose to forgive and let go of hate and anger when we have been wronged. And while this is not for the weak of character, the rewards reaped by those who choose this route are equally as powerful.

Some individuals reading this may feel as though I am minimizing people's pain. Anyone who knows me, however, can tell you that is the opposite of what I stand for. I actually work with people every day with stories similar to these and have nothing but compassion for what they have experienced. In fact, it is exactly why I do what I do. What I never do is pity people. Though it is often confused for love, pity is not love at all. It actually does more harm than good in that it prevents change and keeps people bound to their past.

While pity is indeed pitiful, empathy is extremely powerful. And when I am working with hurting people, empathy always comes through. As a matter of fact, it is not uncommon for me to tell people how sorry I am for what they have gone through. I am someone who understands pain at a very real level. I also deeply understand what it takes to change. For this reason, I always help people steer the conversation away from victimhood and into personal responsibility.

Although this may not always happen right away, I press on, as it is the only way to get to the other side.

Most people with a victim mindset live in self-pity. Self-pity is often at the root of chronic depression and is extremely destructive to our lives. The allure of the pity party is that it offers a way to circumvent personal responsibility. If we can blame anyone but ourselves, we do not have to take ownership of our mistakes. The downside is that pity parties could literally go on forever. I too once loved pity parties, until I learned that God does not attend them. God likes faith parties, praise parties, and victory parties. And He *always* shows up to those.

For those who still have a tendency to host the occasional pity party, though, do not be discouraged. Pity parties are often just another part of the journey of learning how to become an overcomer. Many people become stuck in victim mentality because they do not know any better. For some, it is simply because they were never taught to overcome. Coping with life is taught by example through our family of origin. And if we did not learn it in childhood, then we have to learn it for ourselves as adults.

Others have been so beat down by life and people that they lack the self-confidence to see themselves as overcomers. In addition, there are many people who know they have to change, but have absolutely no clue how to go about that. When we are in a dark pit, it is often very hard to find faith and optimism. But even in the dark pit, when the student becomes ready, life begins to send the teachers who will help them come into the light.

As I move further into this discussion on owning our power of choice, I would be remiss not to bring up the subject of *denial,* as this is a term commonly used with regard to the process of change. Denial is a defense mechanism—a protective and unconscious coping device that allows people to suppress their awareness of a problem in their lives.

Denial is ignoring the pink elephant in the room. It is accepting unacceptable behaviors in our lives. Denial is making excuses for ourselves and/or others. Denial keeps us stuck in the same place because we cannot fix what we don't first acknowledge. To live in denial is to live in deception. Denial opposes truth, and we all know what Jesus said about that: "And you shall know the truth, and the truth shall make you free" (John 8:32 NKJV).

The process of beginning to look at the truth after years of denial and deception, while paramount to change, can be extremely uncomfortable. In addition, most people hate the idea of discomfort. The irony of that, however, is that there cannot be change without discomfort. This reminds me of a coffee mug I own that reads, "Life begins at the end of your comfort zone." The status quo *is* the comfort zone. Thus, all we have to do is examine our lives and ask ourselves if we want things to stay the same. If your answer to that is no, then I tell you the same thing I tell many of my clients: "Get comfortable being uncomfortable for a while."

There is yet another aspect of life that, though common to all, often blurs the lines of personal responsibility. That is disappointment arising from interpersonal relationships. Anger, hurt, betrayal, and the like are powerful emotions that wreak havoc on the lives of many. We may feel entitled, based on the actions of others, to respond or react in dysfunctional ways. And while people can indeed be challenging, the power of choice rests on the fact that, even though we cannot control many things outside ourselves (including others), we can always control our inner world.

How can we do this? By making life-affirming choices. Indeed, when we view it from this perspective, we realize that the power of choice actually sets us free from having to live at the mercy of other people's actions. However, this freedom is well worth the effort it necessitates, as being controlled by what others do is a surefire way to live an unhappy life.

The power of choice is based on the concepts of sowing and reaping and cause-and-effect. It does not focus on what other people are doing, but on how one is responding to what other people are doing. Neither does the power of choice focus on circumstances per se, but on how one is reacting to the circumstances that surround him or her.

Do unfair things happen in this world? Yes. Do people do stupid things? Absolutely. Are people often unreasonable, difficult, and obnoxious? Undeniably. The power of choice posits this question, though: What does that have to do with you and me? Are we so powerless that other people and outside circumstances have that much control over our thoughts, emotions, and actions? The answer to that is no. We are not powerless at all. We are actually extremely powerful, more powerful than we can fathom. The problem is that we constantly give our power away to the slightest little annoyance. And if we cannot handle a slight annoyance, how do you think we will fair in the *actual* problems of life?

More often than not, the reason why people give their power away so easily is because they do not have an understanding of the power of choice. God did not create weak, impulsive, fragile beings. He created us in His image and in His likeness. The problem is that we have been deceived for so long that we have grown to see ourselves as vulnerable to everything around us. People are generally not aware of the inherent power and resources that God has placed inside each of us. In fact, if we humans would awaken to our true God-given potential, this world would be dramatically different.

The power of choice is based on an understanding that life is life and people are people, but each of us gets to choose what we will think, speak, feel, and do. I agree with Charles Swindol in that life is more about how we react to the things that happen to us than about what actually happens to us. We must realize that the manner in which we respond to our circumstances is a choice, albeit an unconscious one. Indeed, the majority of our thought patterns, belief systems, reactions, and responses exist at the unconscious level, below our level of awareness.

Thus, the journey of personal responsibility begins with becoming aware of the impact of our choices. Socrates is quoted as having said that the unexamined life is not worth living. I believe this is precisely what he was talking about—living according to our base instincts; reacting impulsively to the things around us; and having little to no awareness of the fact that we are creating our reality from moment to moment by what we think, speak, feel, and do.

Even if we were victimized as children, as adults we make decisions, and those decisions have consequences. I saw this time and time again during my work with female inmates and victims of domestic violence. As one can imagine, there was some rough history there, and a slew of bad choices. As a result, many of these individuals were stuck in a victim mindset.

In an effort to bring them to the point of personal responsibility, I often challenged them, in love, to consider their own choices. While they had certainly been victimized, in order to move forward they had to take responsibility for their part—whether that was staying in a violent relationship, committing crimes that landed them in prison, or partaking in self-destructive acts that damaged their self-worth. Taking ownership of their part was often the major turning point in their journey of change.

In order to become more conscious of our choices, we have to understand that everything begins in the mind. Indeed, we have all been programmed from the moment of birth by our parents and family of origin, culture, upbringing, and life experiences. Some of this programming has been correct, while a lot of it has been erroneous.

For the purposes of providing clarity to the reader, let me explain how this works. Our five senses act as the gates through which information, or *stimuli*, enters our inner world from our outer world. In order for that stimuli to be interpreted, it must be filtered through the mind. Our *programming* (our fixed belief systems, paradigms, perspectives, and thought patterns) is the filter information must pass through in order to be processed into something that makes sense to us. But what happens if the filter itself is defective or erroneous? In that case, though input may be neutral in nature and quality, once it goes through defective filters, it will produce distorted output. Saying it another way, the filter distorts and changes the nature of the input.

Until we bring conscious awareness to our thinking patterns, this automatic and destructive process will endure uninterrupted. And as a result, we will continue to live the *unexamined life*. One of my favorite quotes on the power of our thoughts is from the book *Eat, Pray, Love*. The book details the story of a woman's quest to find answers pertaining to life.

During the India-leg of her journey, a fellow American, who was also there to study the ancient practice of meditation, said this to her: "You need to learn how to select your thoughts just the same way you select your clothes every day. This is a power you can cultivate. If you want to control things in your life so bad, work on the mind. That's the only thing you should be trying to control" (Gilbert, 2006).

Indeed, learning how to control our minds is truly the beginning of creating the lives we want.

Once we begin to take responsibility for our thoughts, then the next step is to become aware of how our thought lives affect our emotions. Basically, every thought is going to create a same or similar feeling. We cannot think all sorts of negative, unhappy thoughts and expect to feel happy, excited, or peaceful. It just does not work that way. The flipside of that is, of course, that by selecting our thoughts *on purpose*, we also begin to have control over what we feel.

Selecting our thoughts *on purpose* refers to our ability to think with intentionality by choosing the thoughts we wish to think about and releasing those that we don't. As we control our thoughts, we also control our emotions. Consequently, when we begin to have control over our emotions, we are able to control how we feel inside our bodies. We are holistic beings, and what we think and feel affects us physically. Every psychological symptom has a physiological component. This is because we cannot separate our bodies from our feelings and thoughts, and vice versa.

On the contrary, when we begin to use our minds intentionally toward our desired ends, we begin to build the kind of lives we desire. We begin to have control of our inner worlds, which in turn allows us to control our actions and reactions. Our *reactions* represent the ways we typically respond to negative outside stimuli, i.e. offenses from other people, life stressors, problems, etc. This includes the way we speak to people, the choices we make to attempt to solve a problem, and the coping mechanisms (or lack thereof) that we employ.

It is absolutely life-changing to live in the knowledge that we are the masters of our minds and inner worlds. The realization that we can always control what is happening inside ourselves is utterly empowering. Indeed, we have power over our thoughts, feelings, actions, and reactions. And this is not something mystical or difficult to attain. Neither does this mean we enter Nirvana and all the problems of the world and life cease to exist. While it is true that the ability to control our inner world is not a shelter from negative life circumstances, over time it will result in a lot less self-inflicted trouble.

Moreover, owning our power of choice strengthens us on the inside and equips us to deal with the difficult moments in life. Thus, living a life of personal responsibility makes it possible to be happy and peaceful no matter what is happening around us. At the end of the day, happiness is a choice. Overcoming our past is also choice. Forgiveness is another choice. Healing—another choice. Life is indeed full of choices, good ones and bad ones. But there are few neutral ones. So today, own your power of choice. You can start right now if you haven't already.

Know this, though, fellow traveler: however your life turns out, it will be 100 percent on you. Today, be empowered by this notion. I am. Because it means that we can change anything that we do not like about our lives. It means that we can be whoever we want to be in this world. Today, exercise your power of choice. Bask in it. Refuse to give it away. You are not weak, vulnerable, or fragile. You are divinely powerful, and you can do whatever you want to do! It is your choice entirely. So choose wisely.

Lesson 5: Own Your Power of Choice
Questions for Self-reflection

1. What does the power of choice represent to you? How has the information in this chapter helped you to understand it better?

_____

_____

_____

_____

2. Circle the answer that applies to you: My decisions are affected by the actions and opinions of others {always / sometimes / never}.

_____

_____

_____

_____

3. Do you typically have control over your reactions or do you often feel controlled by things happening outside yourself? What tends to trigger a loss of control?

_____

_____

_____

_____

4. List five keys from this chapter for managing your reactions in a better way?

_____

_____

_____

_____

5. What is the connection between our thoughts and our feelings/
    emotions? How will this information help you in the future?

    _____

    _____

    _____

    _____

Lesson 6

Always Expect God's Best

As I have been writing and editing the chapters of this book, I have been surprised by the realization that two themes keep popping up: Number one, the reality that *life is not always easy;* and number two, *life is what we make of it.* Though seemingly contradictory, when we combine these themes with all of the previous lessons, we recognize that they actually go hand in hand. And as we shall see, the lesson of this chapter—*learning to expect the best from God*—is no exception. As a matter of fact, this lesson is crucial to learning how to master the prior ones.

By the time I got to the place in my life where the only logical next step was to have a nervous breakdown, it goes without saying that my perspectives were incredibly warped. I could not think rationally about a lot of things because I had gotten so used to being hurt and disappointed by life. Thankfully, through the process of my spiritual and personal growth journey, I was able to gain insight into the error of many of my belief systems. Early on, my therapist was specifically instrumental in helping me to realize the destructive nature of my negative and derogatory thinking.

Difficult though it was to examine myself so closely, as the good student of life that I had begun to be, I listened. As a result, I was able to become aware of the nature of my negative thinking patterns, most of them directed toward myself. I remember a poignant moment very clearly when my therapist asked me why I felt the need to be so negative. My response was, "If I don't expect anything good, then I won't be disappointed when I don't get what I want." The truth is that I had developed the expectation of not getting what I wanted, and that is usually exactly what I got.

You see, like many people who have been disillusioned by life, I had developed a belief system similar to *reverse psychology*. Whereas reverse psychology is often a strategy people employ in order to manipulate others, I used it as a way to protect myself from future disappointments. By constantly prohibiting positive or hopeful thoughts or preparing myself for the worst, I thought I was being "realistic." I learned, however, that by thinking negatively, I was actually attracting to myself the very things I was hoping to avoid. Today, life has come full circle in that I often hear my own clients verbalize this exact sentiment. Sadly, it is quite common the world over.

This is precisely why there are so many negative people roaming around this world. We all know many of them, don't we? And, truth be told, we want to run in the opposite direction when we see them coming. But the reality is that these pessimists are merely hurting people trying to protect themselves from pain. They simply have not learned that negativity actually makes us our own worst enemy. Indeed, it does not protect us from anything bad at all, but actually has the exact opposite effect—*negativity attracts negative circumstances to our lives and closes doors of opportunity*.

Pessimism is defined as "A feeling or belief that bad things will happen in the future … a feeling or belief that what you hope for will not happen" (Merriam-Webster's Online Dictionary, n.d.). Pessimistic people are individuals who have an expectation of doom and gloom. They are always expecting something bad to happen. They inherently believe that what they want will not come to pass and what they do not want, will. They are generally people who have allowed themselves to become bitter and cynical due to past painful experiences.

Though I thoroughly understand how past hurts can cause us to erect all sorts of walls of protection, I have also learned that everyone in this world has a story of pain. As a counselor and psychotherapist for many years now, I have learned that anyone who tries to could find an excuse to become bitter and cynical. The opposite is also true.

My work at a female prison opened my eyes to this in a big way. I was inspired every day by women who, despite harsh circumstances, were trying to make the best of every day. They were striving to be positive amongst an ocean of negativity. The majority of the women there had suffered a great deal of pain and traumatic life events. Did they have an excuse to be bitter, angry, and negative? You bet they did. And while some of them certainly chose that route, I met so many amazing and inspiring women who did not.

When you have the opportunity to help people through ministry, a counseling practice, or just by being available to the hurting, your heart opens up to the amount of pain that people go through in this life. I have heard it said that every man lives in silent despair. Sadly, many do live in silent despair, albeit unnecessarily.

From children who have been victimized; to adults who still carry the scars of childhood; to marriages in deep trouble and the children who are bearing the brunt of it; to the millions in our own backyard, struggling with debilitating depression and mental illness; to the epidemic of homelessness, addiction, and trauma affecting billions of people—everywhere we turn, people are hurting.

I am not stating these things to be negative, but when I am forced to confront the pain of others, I get a much-needed reality check. It allows me to connect with how blessed I truly am and calls to mind my purpose on the earth. Pessimistic people, on the other hand, are usually self-focused and often possess a victim mindset. They are caught up in obsessive introspection that causes them to perceive their lot as somehow worse than everyone else's. What's worse is that pessimistic people also tend to feel entitled to their misery and subsequent bad behavior. This prevents them from taking responsibility for their actions, thereby also avoiding responsibility for their consequences, i.e. owning their power of choice.

By the same token, I have had the honor of meeting some amazing people along the way, who, in the face of tragedy or great adversity, counted on the grace of God to get them to the other side. They did so with a conviction that they would not only survive, but they would thrive. Indeed, the individuals who fair the best in life are those who find a way to become better people as a result of having gone through pain. They take that pain and make a mission out of it instead of using it as an excuse to check out.

In life, attitude is everything. Our attitudes have a lot to do with our belief systems and the mindsets with which we approach life. This reminds me of something I have heard many times: "Our attitude determines our altitude." Our attitudes can be positive or negative. The way we deal with past hurts or negative circumstances, for example, reveals our true heart attitudes. Do we see ourselves as victims or victors? A success story or a failure? Perspective in these cases is everything. Truly, if we want to be happy, it is the job of every single one of us to deal with and overcome our pasts. This includes not only the things that happened to us that were negative, but also all of the false beliefs and erroneous programming we acquired as a result.

In addition, our belief systems and mindsets affect our self-confidence. If we believe that we can, we are right. If we believe that we can't, we are also right. If we wake up every day already rehearsing in our mind all of the things that can go wrong, we automatically set ourselves up for a bad day.

We have all heard of the *Law of Attraction* and the *Law of Sowing and Reaping*. Basically, these laws dictate that what we think, speak, and do cause a ripple effect somewhere in the cosmos. This ripple effect, in turn, attracts to our lives things that match what we have put out there, thereby returning a similar or same result. Have you ever placed a paperclip close to a magnet? Even Superman cannot keep them from coming together. It happens automatically. That is why it is called a *law*.

So is it with life. We are constantly putting things out there via the thoughts that we think, the words that we say, and the things that we do. But few people live aware of the magnetic attraction those thoughts, words, and actions will have to similar things. It is wishful thinking to believe that we can put whatever we want out there and have good results. The bottom line is this: We cannot live negatively and think we will have a good life. Based on these laws, what we give is what we get, and what we put out there is what comes back to us.

Abraham Lincoln said, "Most folks are as happy as they make up their minds to be." While I wholeheartedly agree with Abe, I am also well aware of the fact that getting to this point is a journey. It is certainly not an easy transition, but I can tell you from experience that it is very possible and absolutely life-changing.

So much has already been said about the power of our thoughts. And yet so much more can be said on the matter. This is because the way we think affects every aspect and area of our lives. Not to mention that there is no way we could ever change our lives without changing the ways we habitually think. Paul could not have made this any clearer than he did in Romans 12:2. Let us, therefore, revisit this powerful verse, but this time from a slightly different perspective:

> Do not be conformed to this world (this age), [fashioned after and adapted to its external, superficial customs], *but be transformed (changed) by the [entire] renewal of your mind [by its new ideals and its new attitude],* so that you may prove [for yourselves] what is the good and acceptable and perfect will of God, even the thing which is good and acceptable and perfect [in His sight for you]. (Romans 12:2 AMP)

It is highly significant to me that Paul is speaking of something as profound as life transformation and only offers one change: our minds. I guess he understood the fundamental truth that escapes many: *When we change our mind, we change everything.*

Indeed, people can be saved for forty years and never experience a true life transformation. In fact, they can die and even go to heaven never having experienced the full benefits of the redeemed life. Why? It's simple: They did not renew their minds. To renew our minds literally means to think with the mind of Christ—to think like Jesus would think, and subsequently speak as He would speak. In the book of Colossians, Paul sheds further light into the manner in which the renewed mind thinks:

> If then you have been raised with Christ [to a new life ...], aim at and seek the [rich, eternal treasures] that are above, where Christ is, seated at the right hand of God. And *set your minds and keep them*

set on what is above (the higher things), not on the things that are on the earth. For [as far as this world is concerned] you have died, and your [new, real] life is hidden with Christ in God. (Colossians 3:1–3 AMP)

To understand the redeemed life is to have a full revelation that we are a new creation. The old pessimistic victim, i.e. the old man, is dead and buried. But it is our responsibility to refuse to think the way he thought and choose to think the way God thinks. How do we know what God thinks? Simple: We think about things as they would exist in heaven. We ask ourselves, "Would this occur in heaven?" Or, "Would Jesus be thinking about this right now?" And if so, "Would He be thinking about it in this way?"

The natural man thinks on lower things (death, disease, lack, fear, etc.), but the spiritual man thinks on the things that are above. Paul delineated some examples of what these *things* are in Philippians 4:8: things that are true, noble, just, pure, lovely, of a good report, virtuous, and praiseworthy (NKJV). Pessimistic people tend to think about the exact opposite of these things and, because we create what we think, the opposite is exactly what they get.

While learning the destructive nature of negativity is absolutely vital for life change, it is also important to note that neutrality is not much better. When a car is in neutral, the engine is running, fuel is being burned, but the car is not going anywhere. So it is when our thoughts are neutral—neither good nor bad. Ceasing negativity is indeed a great first step, but it does not end there. The next step is to put our lives on drive by becoming positive *on purpose*. This is done by first taking responsibility for and interrupting negative thoughts, followed by changing those thoughts into the exact opposite. Next, we choose to think, also on purpose, the way heaven would think on the matter.

And, as if it couldn't get any better, there is a third step even more evolved than the first two. That is to begin to create the life we want by putting *intention* behind our desired outcomes. Intention is a powerful thing. It is the force behind our desires. The intention behind a thought, word, and even a prayer determines how powerful it will be to effect the change we want. Intention refers to the amount of determination, energy, and power we direct toward a desired end and how much of ourselves we put toward our goals and dreams.

Intention involves more than just our thoughts and words. It encompasses our entire personality, our will, and the channeling of our spirit, energy, and inner resources, all intensely directed toward our desires. It is being 100 percent on board, with all of our faculties, about what we want; it requires a resolute rejection of the alternative. It happens in thought, word, and speech, but it mostly takes place in our hearts. When it comes to intention, *why* we do something is much more important than *what* we do.

The opposite is also true. The lack of intention weakens our prayers and sabotages our results. The outcome is often that our prayers and desires fail to manifest. Discrepancies between our words and heart motives negatively impact the intention behind our prayers. We may say we want something, but our heart may not be so sure. Or we may not be fully ready to take the steps necessary to attain what we want. Other times, our faith is the issue. Again, we may say we believe something will happen but, in our heart of hearts, we lack true faith that it actually will. This is why merely paying lip service to something will not make it ours. Indeed, *the power of intention is necessary to create the life that God has for us.*

It is undeniable that when we combine the power of intention with the creative power of our thoughts, words, and actions, we become a force to be reckoned with. This is when all things become possible for an individual. Going after our dreams and goals with intention and positive thinking, declaring the truth of God over our lives, and taking positive steps every day toward our goals will get us to the end that we desire. The power of God and the fullness of his presence within each of us will enable us to accomplish whatever we need to accomplish and overcome whatever we need to overcome. What's more is that by choosing, on purpose, to think and speak like God, we are cooperating with the finished work of Christ and thereby grabbing hold of our inheritance.

Learning and applying these principles has truly transformed my life. Before I started my walk with Jesus, I was riddled with addictions and problems, but I could not find the willpower to change a thing. As I grew in God, He showed me that my destiny was in my own hands. Indeed, I learned that finding God's will for my life was not about desperately seeking Him for it, but about trusting the Christ in me and enabling myself of His indwelling resources.

This revelation has empowered me to become a cocreator with God and has given me a zeal for life. With its endless possibilities, every day is exciting to me. Most days I wake up and say, "Okay, God, what do you have in store for me today?" I am at the edge of my seat as I embark on the journey of each new day. I expect to get my socks knocked off by God, and I usually do.

Does this mean that I never experience negative circumstances? Of course not. This *is* life, after all. The difference is that now when negative things happen, I am emotionally equipped to deal with them because I have not been wasting precious energy on pessimistic thoughts. I spend very little time these days being frustrated by negative things, as I have found this to be an exercise in futility. Instead, I take a solution-oriented approach.

Solution-oriented people deal with problems optimistically and tend to focus on the alternatives for dealing with a problem. Problem-oriented people, on the other hand, spend their time dwelling on the negativity of the problem. This, in turn, causes them to react and respond to their problems in negative ways. Reacting negatively to a problem only serves to amplify the problem and weakens the ability to solve it. Solution-oriented people respond to a problem with faith, a good attitude, alternatives, and problem-solving skills.

Now, while I am aware that some reading this may think that my approach to life is extremely far-fetched for the average person, I will remind you once again that getting here has been *the* journey. I did not get here overnight, and neither will you. In fact, I have been progressively growing toward this for many years. But if it can happen for me, it can certainly happen for you. There is a Buddhist saying that offers some simple and encouraging wisdom in this regard: "The end depends upon the beginning." The key is to start.

Putting these principles into practice will make you a believer, just as it made me a believer. And once you become a believer, you will see that it takes on a life of its own. You will find yourself naturally growing in optimism and expectation of God's best. The more positive you become, the more positive things you will attract. As you continue to attract good things to your life, you will become even more motivated to be positive and expect the best. This, in turn, will make you a magnet for even more blessings. It is a wonderful cycle of ooie gooie goodness.

So today, be encouraged! You have the power within you to create the amazing life that God wants for you. He has fully equipped you with his presence, power, and nature. He has laid out an awesome plan for your life and only has His best in store for you. There is, however, an important caveat one must be aware of when embarking on this journey: *Often the good is the enemy of the best.* Take heart, though, dear sojourner. You can always avoid this trap.

"How?" you ask. By becoming the type of person who will not settle for *anything* but God's best in *every* area of your life. By refusing all other alternatives. By opening your heart to life and its limitless possibilities. By choosing to be happy. And, as you do, the blessings of God will inevitably begin to overtake every aspect of your life. It's just up to you now, friend. So today, begin to expect God's best and nothing but His best. For He has declared you worthy, and who are you to disagree?

Lesson 6: Always Expect God's Best
Questions for Self-reflection

1. Would you say your thoughts tend to be more optimistic or pessimistic?

   _____

   _____

   _____

   _____

2. Do you often find yourself trying to protect yourself from disappointment by expecting the worst? How has this approach hurt you?

   _____

   _____

   _____

   _____

3. When problems arise, do you have a solution-oriented approach or a problem-oriented approach? What can you do to be more solution-oriented?

   _____

   _____

   _____

   _____

4. Based on the information presented in this chapter, what does the *power of intention* mean to you? How does it relate to prayers that have not been answered or desires that have not yet manifested in your life?

   _____

   _____

   _____

   _____

5. What can you start doing differently today to begin to expect the best from God and life?

_____

_____

_____

_____

Lesson 7

Your Character Precedes You

It used to be that a person's character was everything. Indeed, society valued principles such as honesty and integrity even over prosperity, wealth, and success. Individuals cared what others thought of them and sought to protect their reputations in their dealings with other people. The collective good often overpowered the individual good. And people based their choices on their value systems and character, more so than on getting what they wanted.

Sadly, over the years there has been a gradual eroding of these ideals, as we have traded in values that safeguard society for values that ensure prosperity and career success. Although we penalize moral failures explicitly, we often encourage them implicitly. However, when the safeguards meant to bring balance and well-being to society begin to crumble, society itself is not far behind.

We have all heard the old adage, "Your reputation precedes you." Years ago, people emphasized the importance of their *names*, which were synonymous with their *reputations*. We see evidence of this dating back to our beloved Bible stories, many of which documented the experiences of individuals who had profound encounters with God. Not surprisingly, an encounter with God often brought about a drastic life change. What may come as a surprise to some, however, is the fact that along with that life change came a change in that person's perception of self and purpose for living.

It is for this reason that in many of these stories God changed the names of the individuals to make them more in line with their new nature and purpose. Past generations fundamentally understood the wisdom of protecting one's reputation and character. And the fact that we have moved away from this does not bode well for the future of our world.

Today, the overall mentality has shifted more toward hedonism and selfish ambitions. We compete with one another to see who can die with the most toys. What's more is that the effects of this mentality are evident in the way our current generation is viewed. Today's generation is often referred to as *the Entitlement Generation*. The reason for this unsavory label is that they want everything their parents worked hard to obtain, but with little to no effort.

Entitlement refers to the belief that one deserves everything in life, just because. As a psychotherapist, I have come to find that entitlement is among the most destructive personality traits operating in people's lives. Entitlement sabotages an individual's ability to grow and overcome character and personality issues, because entitled people have difficulty taking responsibility for their actions. For entitled people, everything is always someone else's fault.

Unfortunately, there is a great deal of entitlement in people these days. There is also a lot of pressure to get ahead. Not to mention the fact that life has become harder as the cost of living has consistently been on the rise. As a result, our priorities and values have been steadily shifting toward an emphasis on self. The combination of all of these factors, as well as other factors not mentioned, has brought about a change in the ways we conduct our professional and personal interactions. This change has not added to, but taken away from us as a society. That is why I believe it is time for us to begin again to teach and emphasize the importance of character and integrity.

There is a powerful quote by an unknown author that I have heard and used myself many times: "Watch your thoughts; they become your words. Watch your words; they become your actions. Watch your actions; they become your habits. Watch your habits; they become your character. Watch your character, because it will be your destiny."

This powerful quote aptly depicts the automatic process that is always taking place in our lives. Like a domino effect, it begins with a thought, which will eventually become a spoken word. Whatever we think and speak, we will eventually act on. Actions that are repeated become habits. Human beings are creatures of habit. And the ways in which we habitually think, speak, and act begin to form our reputation with others. In turn, our reputation and life choices create our destiny from moment to moment.

As we have already learned from previous chapters, for every action, there is a reaction. For every cause, there is an effect. Everything that we say and do is like a boomerang going out before us and springing back toward us, causing some sort of result. Truly, the amount of power we have to create our reality cannot be underestimated. Neither can the roles that our character and reputation play in all of this.

A lot of people live unaware of this phenomenon, however, since the consequences of our actions do not always happen right away. In fact, we may not experience the results for a week, a month, or even a year. But they will come. Similarly, a life of compromise typically takes an insidious progression, often unconscious to an individual until it is too late. People do not wake up one day and suddenly do something horrible. More often than not, small compromises become bigger and bigger, slowly taking over their entire lives and personalities.

At the end of the day, we really do not fool anyone. Eventually people see exactly who we are. And eventually what is hidden comes to the light (Luke 8:17 NKJV). Every day, we see the consequences of compromise strewn all over the news for all to see: the politician wrought with scandal, the businessman caught with his hand in the proverbial cookie jar, the spiritual giant fallen from grace. As painful as these experiences are for those involved, they tell a cautionary tale we would all be wise to heed: *Our character and reputation precede us.*

To *precede* means to go before (Merriam-Webster's Online Dictionary, n.d.). It also speaks of the heralding or conveying of news or information. Furthermore, *character* is defined as "The way someone thinks, feels, and behaves; someone's personality; one of the attributes or features that make up and distinguish an individual" (Merriam-Webster's Online Dictionary, n.d.). When we put these definitions together, we can see a picture of *character* emerging.

Our character represents the way that our personality and values are reflected to others through our dealings and interactions with them. It embodies the characteristics and attributes specific to us. A person's character can be positive or negative. We can reflect exceptional character, poor character, or anything in between. In sum, our character carries information about us for the world to see, whether we realize it or not.

Moreover, what drives our character is our value system. Indeed, what we value, we prioritize. Jesus stated, "For where your *treasure* is there your *heart* will be also" (Matthew 6:21 NKJV). This short verse conveys powerful implications as it pertains to the course our lives will naturally take on. In addition, the order of the words *heart* and *treasure* are extremely significant to the context. Here *heart* represents our lives and desires, while *treasure* represents our priorities—the things we value in life.

It is clear from the context that it is our values and priorities that direct our lives and hearts, and not the other way around. In other words, what we value, we prioritize, and what we prioritize directs and defines our choices. Another way to look at this is by exploring our *time, treasure, and talents*. If we want to know where our real values and priorities lie, we can find out by examining where the majority of our time (time and energy), treasure (money and resources), and talents (abilities and passions) are spent.

This examination of our time, treasure, and talents can help us to be honest with ourselves regarding our priorities and values. More important, it is foundational for our mental health and well-being. Undoubtedly, hypocrisy is a great source of mental illness and dysfunction in people's lives. It is acting outside of our intrinsic values, making choices we detest, and pretending to be someone we are not. Hypocritical people will act one way outwardly, but inwardly will think or feel the opposite. Whether they realize it or not, this takes a profound toll on their lives and relationships. The truth is that while we may think we are benefiting by taking shortcuts and making compromises, in reality, the costs far outweigh the gains.

This is something I too had to learn in my walk with Jesus. Like so many people, I was oblivious to how deeply ingrained dishonesty was in me. That was, of course, until I started owning my power of choice. Before my nervous breakdown, it was all too common for me to use deception and manipulative tactics to get my way. As God changed my heart, though, those compromises became increasingly foreign and uncomfortable to me.

I did not want to be that person anymore, so I became accountable to myself, others, and God for my actions. As I did, great changes started taking place—not only *within* me, but *without*. I experienced increased success, both personally and professionally. Not to mention that the more I practiced honesty in my behaviors, the more of God's goodness I witnessed in my life. Thus, I learned a fundamental truth of God—*good always wins out in the end*.

Indeed, there is tremendous power in honesty and truth. Jesus said, "And you shall know the truth, and the truth shall make you free (John 8:32 NKJV)." As a matter of fact, honesty is the foundational hallmark of exceptional character. Honesty does not just represent telling the truth, though it certainly includes that. It represents a desire to live honestly and authentically in all of our affairs. It is more than not lying to people or cheating on our taxes. It is about being someone that others can trust and believe. Honesty is truly refreshing in a world where people so often tell you what they think you want to hear, even if it is a flat out lie. Moreover, honesty is a belief system and lifestyle, more than it is an individual act.

An honest person values the truth and cares about people enough not to lie to them. Sometimes the truth is inconvenient. Sometimes it will cause people to reject or persecute us. But honesty means telling the truth even when it is uncomfortable or inconvenient to do so. I, for one, am where I am today because of honest people, who told me what I *needed* to hear, not necessarily what I *wanted* to hear. In addition, honesty often means allowing ourselves to be vulnerable—sharing our true feelings and inner selves with other people. Lastly, honesty provokes trust in others, which opens doors in every area of our lives. People greatly admire honesty; they are drawn to honesty. Thus, having the reputation of being honest will take us very far in life.

Another great hallmark of a person of exceptional character is *integrity*. Integrity is doing the right thing because it *is* the right thing. Like honesty, it is more a principle for life than an act. One is either a person of integrity or not. Indeed, one or various integral acts do not make a person of integrity, but an individual's mindsets, beliefs, and consistent actions—personally and professionally—do.

A person of integrity does the right thing even when no one is looking. Actually, an integral person knows that God is always looking and wants to please Him. To the integral person, the opinions that matter most are her own and God's. What's more, integrity is rooted in honesty but goes deeper than honesty in word and deed. It is a value system that emphasizes being an individual whose inside matches her outside.

There is therefore no discrepancy between the actions and personality of a person of integrity. They are who they say they are. As a result, hypocrisy fundamentally repels people of integrity, both in themselves and others. Morally, integral people cannot do things that go against their values, nor do they live to impress others. Ultimately, the actions of people of integrity represent who they are, not what they do.

Yet another characteristic of exceptional character is *consideration for others*. What's more, this principle has at its core the principles of honesty and integrity. It's unfortunate, but if I had a nickel for every time I have interacted with inconsiderate people, I could retire to an island and never have to work another day.

Considerate people fundamentally care about others. They consider how their actions will affect another person before making a choice, as opposed to selfish people, whose main priority is themselves. Selfish people do not generally concern themselves with how their choices will affect others, at least not enough to change their actions. Considerate people, on the other hand, tend to live by the golden rule, "Do unto others as you would have done unto you." They often put themselves in the shoes of another and tailor their decisions accordingly.

It is also noteworthy that being considerate is not synonymous with being a doormat or living a sacrificed life. It is about understanding the fundamental truth that we are all connected. Our actions affect other people and vice versa. While that does not mean that our actions will never negatively impact others, it does mean we care enough to take it into consideration. When our actions do affect others adversely, we take responsibility. As mature individuals, we communicate our apologies and work together to find an agreement. For at the root of consideration is a heart that deeply thinks of and cares about others.

Another staple of exceptional character is being true to our word. Like the aforementioned qualities, this one overlaps with all of the others. When we are true to our word, we are honest, integral, and considerate. Being true to our word is meaning what we say and saying what we mean. It is caring enough about people to avoid misleading them. In fact, one hundred years ago, a person's word was as binding as a document drafted in an attorney's office. The irrefutable truth is that our reputations are greatly impacted by our ability to keep our word. As a result, every time we say we will do something and neglect to do it, our character takes a hit.

Hence, people lose their ability to trust us with every idle word that comes out of our mouths. Indeed, our words carry more weight when people can trust us; they carry less weight when the opposite is true. When an honest person, known to be true to his word, speaks, people listen. Conversely, when a dishonest person speaks, he is not taken seriously. Consequently, being honest and true to our word directly impacts our ability to succeed in life. If people cannot trust us, they will not want us on their team. On the contrary, when we have the trust of others, opportunities tend to fall in our laps.

The last characteristic of exceptional character I will be discussing in this book is by no means least. It is the principle of *excellence*. Excellence is often jumbled together with perfectionism. But excellence is not perfectionism at all. As a matter of fact, the main emphasis of excellence is not on performance per se, but on the effort we put toward something and the attitude with which we do it. While striving for excellence is completely possible, perfection is a trap that is impossible to attain. Indeed, mistakes cannot be avoided and are a normal part of learning and growing. In addition, perfectionism leads to frustration and self-deprecation, whereas excellence leads to self-love, progress, and success.

Having a spirit of excellence is about doing our best and putting our best foot forward. It is about taking pride in what we do because the quality of our work reflects who we are—*and whose we are.* It is possessing an understanding that what we do impacts the way that people perceive us. Excellence in us causes other people to be drawn to us.

Excellence is important in all areas of life, but at the professional level, it is absolutely paramount to moving ahead. In any organization, you will find people who are committed to excellence and others who *phone it in* (do the minimum that they need to do to collect a paycheck). In fact, what sets excellent professionals apart is that they *lead from where they are*—they do more than the minimum without being asked because excellent people see a need and meet it. And not just because they are getting paid to do so, but because excellence rights wrongs.

A former mentor and teacher in this regard always encouraged me to leave every place better than it was when I arrived. This advice has proven to be invaluable to me. Undeniably, my commitment to excellence has wrought much success in all areas of my life and opened many doors in my career. Everything that I do now, I do with passion and gusto, two fundamental qualities of excellent people. Additionally, I always strive to give 100 percent to what I do. As a result, others are drawn to my energy and want me on board.

During my time in the workforce, I have had the honor of working in a variety of organizations. And in every one, my character and professionalism have preceded me. This has resulted in more promotions and opportunities than I have known what to do with. When my season has been over at each workplace, people have always been sad to see me go. I have left a good name for myself in every establishment. And the doors just keep on opening.

Here again, we see the principle of cause-and-effect at work. Whether it is business, ministry, or our personal lives, what we put out there is exactly what comes back to us. Thus, people who get promoted and have doors opened to them are people who have gained the trust and favor of others. People of excellence are trusted, not only because they conduct their activities with honesty and integrity, but also for the exceptional quality of their work.

Truly, trust elicits favor. This is a message that would go a long way in Christian circles to bring deeper understanding as to the favor of God. All too often, there is great emphasis on the expectation of God's favor, with little to no emphasis on the necessary life change that accompanies it. Though people may be shocked to realize it, this is not how the favor of God works. Surely, God knows better than anyone that a weak character cannot sustain His immeasurable blessings. For this reason, He consistently calls us upward and deals with the things in us that are not of Him.

Immaturity and compromise are two such things, as they only threaten to destroy the plan of God for our lives. We cannot expect the favor of God in our endeavors and reflect a poor character. After all, it is Jesus that we represent. And there has never been anyone more excellent than He. Neither is Christianity a short cut to prosperity and success. But it is a higher road of love for God and others. It is precisely on this road that we find our destiny and everything we need to carry it out. There is, therefore, no room for liars, cheaters, or thieves. They have their own road, and it is marked with struggle and pain.

Today, know that God has chosen nothing but His very best for you. But it is only found on this higher road of love and life. Today, choose the high road. Allow the Holy Spirit to make you into the person of character and integrity that you were created to be. Know, however, that God does not want to leave any stone unturned in your life. Truly, you were created for absolute wholeness. And He will not stop until you experience His abundant life in every aspect of your being.

There is one last cautionary detail I would like to share with you, dear reader: As you embark on this journey of change, be prepared to have your mind blown. Though you will most certainly experience unprecedented blessings in your life, what will truly blow your mind is the realization that with each passing day, you are looking more and more like Jesus. And I don't know about you, but I can't imagine any journey more beautiful or powerful than this.

> Nevertheless when one turns to the Lord, the veil is taken away. Now the Lord is the Spirit; and where the Spirit of the Lord is, there is liberty. But we all, with unveiled face, *beholding as in a mirror the glory of the Lord, are being transformed into the same image from glory to glory*, just as by the Spirit of the Lord. (2 Corinthians 3:16–18 NKJV).

Lesson 7: Your Character Precedes You
Questions for Self-reflection

1. What evidence do you see in the world that our values have shifted from protecting our character and reputation to selfish ambitions and getting ahead?

_____

_____

_____

_____

2. Do you see that at all evident in your own life? If so, how?

_____

_____

_____

_____

3. Has life taught you that compromising to get ahead only thwarts our growth and success down the line? List two times when you reaped rewards from choosing the more difficult path of integrity over the easier path of compromise.

_____

_____

_____

_____

4. Has there been hidden or habitual dishonesty in your life? Can you pinpoint evidence that fear was at the root of that dishonesty?

_____

_____

_____

_____

5. Based on this chapter, what characteristics make someone a person of integrity?

_____

_____

_____

_____

Lesson 8

The Art of the Present Moment

There is no doubt about it: humans are a busy bunch. If you are one such human, then one of the biggest gifts you can give yourself is learning to live fully in the present moment. And as the title of this book suggests, it is truly an art. Just as any art needs to be developed, so too do we need to develop our ability to live in and fully experience the present. Certainly, this can be challenging in our day and age, as there are often many obstacles to present moment awareness.

Indeed, at any instant, there are multiple things vying for our attention. For this reason, it is easy to be distracted in this world. Distraction takes place in the mind and creates a disconnect between what we are experiencing and the present moment. The result is a mind that is constantly running and thinking about multiple things at the same time. If we are not careful, this frenzy of busyness and overstimulation can cause our minds to live in a perpetual state of overdrive.

The conscious mind—that is, the working mind—is a constant stream of thoughts. In other words, the process of thoughts entering the mind is often involuntary in nature. We cannot always control the thoughts that come into our conscious mind, though over time, we *can* change the types of thoughts we habitually think. In addition, we can learn to control the thoughts that we choose to entertain. Herein lies the answer to the problem so common to the twenty-first-century individual: the racing mind.

The racing mind is a distracted mind, consumed with many random thoughts, often at the same time. The mind races for hours on end due to the fact that most people do not have a gatekeeper in their mind. As a result, they entertain anything and everything that makes its way into the conscious stream of their thinking. This inability to monitor their thoughts from moment to moment results in a distracted, cluttered, and often out-of-control mind.

Thus, learning to monitor our minds and free them of distractions is the key to mastering the art of the present moment. The truth is that most people spend much of their time thinking about the regrets of the past or the fears of the future. They live burdened by worries of things that will probably never happen. They ruminate on events that previously transpired, to the point of distorting reality. I refer to this mental condition as *living in our heads*.

The truth is that we can either live in our heads or live in the present moment, but we cannot do both. When we are living in our heads, we are habitually engrossed in thought and constantly pulled away from the present by our thought patterns. Our attention is not on what we are *experiencing*, but on what we are *thinking*. Thus we must realize that, in this state, whatever is going on in our minds is not necessarily reality. Actually, more often than not, it is very far from it.

Nevertheless, the allure to retreat to our inner world is, in fact, very real. This is a process that takes place due to many years of allowing our thoughts to go unchecked. It is the result of a mind that has never been disciplined. The draw, of course, is the false comfort that this mental escape affords. Indeed, mentally manipulating the facts and excessively thinking about problems gives people a sense of control, albeit a false one.

Truly, there is so much of life that we simply cannot control. And for many, life's unknowns bring a great deal of fear and anxiety. In an effort to override and quell those fears, people often turn to obsessive ruminations about the problem, as if by doing so they can add to the solution or somehow control the outcome. Neither of these is true. In actuality, worry and fear only hinder our ability to problem-solve by cluttering our minds with negativity, thereby debilitating us emotionally. As this happens, our ability to channel our inner resources toward a problem is impaired and thus greatly diminished.

A cluttered mind is also public enemy number one when it comes to the practice of the present moment. Our culture does a funny thing sometimes—it gives hip terms to something that is dysfunctional and destructive. One such term is *multitasking*. In reality, the human mind was created by God to focus on one thing at a time. In today's world, however, this is seen as the epitome of inefficiency. Nevertheless, as we will see in the proceeding lines, *multitasking mentality* is not only flawed in its logic but also counterproductive.

While we may be under the illusion that productivity is increased when we are thinking about and doing multiple things at once, the opposite is actually true. In fact, multitasking diminishes the quality of our output substantially. Logically speaking, if we are giving our attention to one thing but are interrupted by ten other things, what percentage of our intellectual resources are actually being channeled toward that task? Wouldn't our focus be better served by giving 100 percent toward one thing, then 100 percent toward the next, and so on?

Unfortunately, productivity is not the only thing affected by multitasking mentality. Our relationships also take a major hit under this global farce. I witnessed a sad example of this between a teen and his mom one day while exercising outdoors. Walking side-by-side, mom had her attention turned toward her smartphone while her son walked in silence. Suddenly, in a classic "out of the mouth of babes" moment, the teen turned toward his mother and exclaimed, "Mom! Why do you always have to be on your phone? You can't even talk to me when we are out here walking together!" Not only was I saddened by the fact that the teen had to call his mom out on this, but that mom was too caught up to realize the beauty of the moment she was allowing to slip by.

Without a doubt, life is only truly lived in the present moment. One of my favorite sayings on this matter is, "Yesterday is history, tomorrow is a mystery, and today is a gift—that's why we call it the present." In actuality, the only thing that is real *is* the moment. As much as we might regret things that happened in the past, it is over. As much as there is uncertainty about the future, it is not here yet. Indeed, neither of them is relevant to the *now*. But having a mind distracted by regrets, fears, multitasking, and/or the beeping and buzzing of technology hurts our ability to enjoy life to the fullest. *Simply put, when we are not present, we miss so much.* It is only when we are fully awake and alert to the present moment that we can experience the fullness of life.

God Himself is accessed and can only be fully experienced in the present moment. He is not in the past, and He is not in the future, as neither of those exists. In fact, it is through our awareness of the present that we are able to be in tune with His abiding presence and intervention in our day-to-day lives. Thus, we even miss so much of God when we choose our inner world over our present reality. Jesus clearly understood this. And He felt so strongly about it that He covered it in his famous teaching series commonly referred to as *the Sermon on the Mount*: "So do not worry or be anxious about tomorrow, for tomorrow will have worries and anxieties of its own. Sufficient for each day is its own trouble" (Matthew 6:34 AMPC).

One might interpret these verses as Jesus stating that we should live in expectation of problems. But that is not at all the case. He was merely stating the senselessness of worrying about tomorrow's *possible* problems today. Upon examination, human nature reveals that we were only created to deal with twenty-four hours at a time. Thus, each moment requires our undivided attention in order to be experienced to the fullest. And as previously stated, thinking about things outside of the present moment causes our minds to become overwhelmed with information. When our minds are overwhelmed, attention is also impaired, which in turn diminishes the function of our memories. I call this state of being *living on autopilot*.

People who live on autopilot basically live unconscious and unaware. They go through their day-to-day lives and fulfill their daily tasks in a weakened state of consciousness. Living in their heads, their attention and ability to focus on the moment is significantly decreased. When people live on autopilot, they make decisions of which they are not fully conscious. They are not giving adequate detail to what they are doing or why they are doing it. Under these conditions, many poor choices with lasting consequences are made. Though few people realize it, much of the dysfunction in their lives is the result of making life choices on autopilot.

Like the example of the mom and her teen on the walking track, when we live on autopilot, we also miss out on experiencing relationships to the fullest. When we are on autopilot, we are not paying due attention to the people around us. We may hear the words that people say, but we often miss the message of their hearts. To be in tune to people, we have to pay attention and really listen to what they are saying. We cannot listen to the chatter in our heads and other people at the same time, at least not effectively.

When I was learning the art of the present moment in my own life, I came across an article that I found helpful. In it, the author gave an example of an individual who wanted to hang a picture frame on her wall. It contrasted the act of doing so awake and alert as opposed to doing so with a distracted mind, i.e. on autopilot. Present moment awareness refers to the ability to *be with* whatever we are doing. So, if that happens to be hanging a frame, *be with* the frame. *Be with* the nail. *Be with* the hammer. Experience yourself holding the hammer tightly as you drive the nail into the wall. Experience yourself hanging the frame on the wall and then be sure to take the time to appreciate a job well done.

Some people reading this may think it quite silly to emphasize the importance of being present to hang a picture frame. However, what is really important here is what the picture frame represents: *all of the little miracles and special moments we stand to miss on a daily basis.* Since living in the present is a lifestyle more than a momentary choice, we cannot pick and choose what we will be present for and what we will be on autopilot for. Living with a distracted mind will undoubtedly cause us to miss out on life events we would want to fully experience. Today it may be a picture frame, but tomorrow it may be a precious interaction with your child, a powerful God-moment, or an act of kindness by your spouse.

Others make the argument that living on autopilot shields us from experiencing the intensity of life's painful moments. There is certainly truth to this, and, trust me, I get the desire to avoid pain. Thing is, I have learned it is impossible to do so, and attempting it only makes matters worse. Suppressed feelings get stored in our soul and body, causing emotional problems and dysfunction. Living in the present allows us to feel what we are feeling and then release it. In fact, pent-up emotions and unresolved issues are at the heart of the mental illness epidemic in our society. Many people live terrified of feeling their feelings as if doing so will open a Pandora's box, never to be shut again. In actuality, it is the avoidance of feelings that we should fear. Life is not about suppressing things that happened to us; it is about overcoming and thereby transcending them.

Consequently, present moment awareness is paramount to healthy emotional expression and release. For this reason, it is greatly emphasized when people are dealing with addictive behaviors or painful life situations. "A day at a time" is a foundational principle in overcoming addictions. It is a lifesaver for individuals who cannot fathom the notion of abstaining from their substance of choice *forever*. In early recovery, individuals learn that they can remain abstinent a moment at a time, but often not more. Yet it is that initial success from moment to moment that eventually leads to a lifetime of freedom.

Similarly, when an individual is coping with the agonizing loss of a loved one, the reality of their new normal can be overwhelming. Thinking ahead brings extreme dread and pain. The present moment offers them a reprieve from the fear of the future without their loved one. The truth is that in the moment, all is well. We may not have everything we want, but we have what we need. Indeed, when life is really hard, the only thing that allows us to put one foot in front of the other is staying in the safety and security of *right now*.

Although tough moments in life cannot be avoided, learning to enjoy the simple delights and blessings of the present somehow makes the difficult times okay. Does it make sense to forgo the many beautiful moments and experiences that life has to offer to prevent a few negative ones? I don't believe so.

My philosophy for life is this: I expect the best out of life. I take life by the horns and seek to live each day to the fullest. At the same time, I accept the reality that life is life and stuff happens. But, because I know that God is in my every moment, I am ready to deal with whatever comes down the pike. Life has grown me up and taught me coping skills. I do not have to be afraid of life. What's more, I can embrace the lesson behind everything, even the negative things that take place.

To many, this may sound great in theory, but the practical application of present moment awareness can indeed be baffling. That is because learning to live in the present moment is simple, but not easy. It is simple because there isn't much to it. It is difficult because it will require consistency and conscious effort. Human beings tend to resist the part that has to do with them, but the truth is that in all of these principles and lessons, there is one common denominator—you and me.

In order to develop the art of the present moment, we must train our minds to focus on the moment and live in the present. We do this by being the gatekeepers of our thoughts. For example, when you find yourself regretting the past or fearing the future, bring your conscious awareness back to the moment and remind yourself that neither of those exists. Remind yourself that the present is the only thing that is real.

Likewise, when you find yourself being constantly interrupted by competing stimuli, choose, on purpose, which one you will focus on—*and choose wisely.* Don't forgo something real and fulfilling, like relationships with others, for devices and virtual reality. At first, you might have to do this a million times a day, but practice makes perfect. And before you know it, present moment awareness will be *your* new normal.

Another important aspect of present moment awareness that cannot be overemphasized is the mind-body-spirit connection. We are holistic beings, but we have the tendency to compartmentalize our existence. We have the perspective that our minds are separate from our emotions, which are separate from our bodies, which are separate from our spirits. But even though these are different aspects of our beings, they work in tandem as part of a whole.

Too often, people report feeling disconnected from their bodies—a sure sign they are living in their heads. Thus, a key aspect of living in the present is the ability to connect with what our bodies are experiencing. Connecting with our senses is a great way to do this. For example, learn to *take in* what your eyes are seeing; *feel* what your hands are touching; *experience* the ground holding you up beneath your feet; *enjoy* the sounds being captured by your ears; and *connect* with the abiding presence of God within your spirit. These are all things that we miss to a large degree when we attempt to live life in our heads.

Allow me to give you an example of how this works by using something most Americans do every day. So imagine that you are drinking a hot, fresh café latte. If you are on autopilot, you may scarf it down in about ten minutes. Absent-mindedly sipping away, you neglect to realize how the simple act of drinking coffee affects your entire being.

Now imagine you are doing the same thing, only this time, all of your senses are engaged. Grabbing hold of the mug, you are immediately comforted by the feel of its warmth at your fingertips. This common feeling sends a message to your brain telling it to relax. As this happens, you can literally feel tight muscles give way to relaxation. Breathing in ever so deeply, you find yourself sinking back into the chair. Next, you do what any self-respecting coffee drinker would do—you raise the mug to your nose and give it a good whiff.

Instantly, its rich aroma hits your scent receptors—and apparently your vocal chords, as you notice an all-too-familiar sound emanating from none other than *you*. *"Mmmmm …"* Sinking deeper still into the chair, you feel your body relaxing all the more. Subsequently, and virtually on impulse, a smile of satisfaction shoots across your face.

Raising the mug once again to your lips, you prepare for your first sip. Immediately you are struck by its tantalizing warmth. You experience a taste explosion in your mouth as coffee, milk, sugar, and cinnamon combine to perfection. Repeating this wonderful cycle, for fifteen minutes you get to sit there, basking in the quiet of the morning or midafternoon. You did not just enjoy your coffee; you fully experienced it. Now that's how you drink coffee, folks!

I can only assume that, to some, my coffee-drinking experience may have seemed overly sensual. Perhaps it is because you have not yet awakened to the amount of pleasure that can be derived from everyday things. Indeed, life is a smorgasbord of delight and pleasure. And learning to enjoy its daily delectations is yet another aspect that makes living it amazing. Not to mention that it gives God great joy to make us happy. After all, it is He who created the human spirit, soul, and body. And I don't think He made any mistakes.

So today, make sure to enjoy every aspect of your life. Begin to awaken to the pleasure in things you have previously taken for granted. As you do, you will suddenly find yourself experiencing so much more enjoyment from life.

Today, don't begrudge the present moment. Embrace it. Enjoy it to the fullest. It is God's gift to you. In it, you will find peace. In it, you will find contentment. In it, you will find all of the little miracles awaiting you around every corner. Know too, dear reader, that by embracing the moment, you are fully embracing life. And as Arthur Rubenstein so aptly put it, as you love life, it will love you right back.

Lesson 8: The Art of the Present Moment
Questions for Self-reflection

1. List three keys to practicing the art of the present moment in your day-to-day life.

   _____

   _____

   _____

   _____

2. What belief systems cause you to fear uncertainty?

   _____

   _____

   _____

   _____

3. Are you often consumed with either regrets from the past or fears of the future? How does that affect your life?

   _____

   _____

   _____

   _____

4. Do you often find yourself living *on autopilot*? If so, what causes you to do so, and what can you do differently in order to live more aware in your day-to-day life?

   _____

   _____

   _____

   _____

5. In what ways has a lack of present moment awareness affected your relationships?

_____

_____

_____

_____

Lesson 9

Let Peace be the Umpire in Your Life

> *And let the peace* (soul harmony which comes) from Christ rule *(act as an umpire* continually) in your hearts *[deciding and setting with finality all questions that arise in your minds,* in that peaceful state] to which as [members of Christ's] one body you were also called [to live]. (Colossians 3:15 AMPC)

I love this verse from the Amplified Bible, Classic Edition. Here the word *umpire,* used metaphorically, gives a vivid depiction of the power behind the peace of God. An umpire in a baseball game is the referee—the person responsible for making the decisions as to which plays will be allowed and which ones will be prohibited. Like a referee, the principle of peace can operate as an umpire in our lives when we have to make difficult decisions.

Many people lack the peace of God in their lives, mostly because they do not fully understand what it is. Let us then begin with a simple definition of *peace.* Merriam-Webster's Online Dictionary defines *peace* in this way: "A state of tranquility or quiet; freedom from disquieting or oppressive thoughts or emotions; harmony in personal relations" (n.d.).

From a natural perspective, peace is a feeling within us. It is a state of tranquility and relaxation that we feel inside our bodies and experience in our minds. From this perspective, *serenity* could also be seen as a synonym for peace—*a state of being calm or peaceful* (Merriam-Webster's Online Dictionary, n.d.).

We have all heard the famous and profound words of Jesus regarding peace: "Peace I leave with you, My peace I give to you; *not as the world gives do I give to you.* Let not your heart be troubled, neither let it be afraid" (John 14:27 NKJV). The depth and power behind these words is not necessarily in the words themselves, but in the distinction that Jesus is drawing between the peace that the world has to offer and the peace that He gives us. For the purposes of this discussion, it is therefore accurate to state that, from a Biblical standpoint, we are referring to *the fruit of the Spirit of peace*:

> But the fruit of the Spirit is love, joy, *peace*, longsuffering, kindness, goodness, faithfulness, gentleness, self-control. Against such there is no law. (Galatians 5:22–23 NKJV)

Every Christian on the planet has been exposed to teachings regarding the fruits of the Spirit. But a deeper understanding as to what the fruits of the Spirit actually are will profoundly impact how we live our lives. The fruits of the Spirit are not things we do or experience per se. They are, literally speaking, aspects of God's divine nature living within each and every one of us. Indeed, love, joy, peace, patience, kindness, goodness, faithfulness, gentleness, and self-control are not things that God *does*; they represent who He *is*.

For this reason, every single person is fully equipped to live the *redeemed life* (overcome our difficulties, transcend our pasts, grow in the character of Jesus, and fulfill our destinies). And not because of anything *we* did, but because of what *Jesus* did. Every believer is a New Creation in Christ (2 Corinthians 5:17 NKJV). The moment we were born again, we were given a new nature—*His nature.* In addition to this, we also received the Holy Spirit, who is the fullness of God's presence and power living on the inside of us. The Holy Spirit is a package deal. In Him we have authority, power, and the fruit and gifts of the Spirit.

Moreover, when we came to Christ, He cleaned up our mess, forgave our sins, and accredited to us His own righteousness. Truly, everything that was against us, He moved out of the way so that we could be who we were created to be from the beginning (Colossians 2:14 NKJV). There is therefore no reason under the sun why any child of God should fail to fulfill the plan of God for his or her life.

The fruits of the Spirit are crucial when it comes to fulfilling our destiny. In fact, each fruit of the Spirit accomplishes different functions in our lives. And the fruit of the Spirit of peace is one that is particularly important in helping to lead our lives in a spiritual and supernatural direction. Additionally, it is absolutely necessary if we are to live well and finish our race. We must therefore break free from the notion that peace is merely a feeling.

If you are like me, at least at one point in your life, you have experienced the absence of peace. Every single day prior to the day I met Jesus was laden with chaos and conflict. Conflict within begets conflict without. Thus was my constant reality. But because it was a common state for me, I was prevented from realizing what I was missing. That was, until I began experiencing the peace of God for myself.

So often we emphasize obtaining the realities of God through self-effort and harsh discipline. I have found this to be not only be self-deprecating but an exercise in futility. After all, it is counter-intuitive to attempt to *obtain* things that are already ours. Thus, growing in Christ is not about obtaining anything *outside* of us, but about developing everything already *in* us. Jesus delivered the best news of all when He said, "It is finished!" (John 19:30 NKJV). By giving us a new nature and identity and placing everything we would need on the inside of us, He put an end, once and for all, to the struggle to obtain—a struggle that has frustrated humanity since the fall of man.

Some of you may be wondering, "What does all of this have to do with peace?" I'm getting there. Truly, it is impossible to help individuals understand how to develop the peace of God in their lives, without first explaining why and how the cross changed everything. Jesus said to His disciples: "It is to your advantage that I go away; for if I do not go away, the Helper will not come to you; but if I depart, I will send Him to you" (John 16:7 NKJV).

The Holy Spirit living in us makes abiding in the supernatural peace of God possible. As a matter of fact, it is supposed to be our natural, normal state. Like the world's peace, God's peace also provides feelings of calm and tranquility, but it does not end there. Indeed, God's peace is a state of being that transcends the emotional level and engulfs our entire being.

When Jesus said that the peace He gives is unlike the world's peace, it is because the world's peace is dependent upon circumstances. Take the average person, for example. They may be seemingly happy and relaxed one moment, but throw a curveball in their day and watch the *façade* of peace quickly fade away. *Jesus's peace, on the other hand, does not diminish in the face of circumstances because it is not dependent on circumstances; it is abiding (meaning, always with us).*

Furthermore, it is written on various occasions that Jesus calmed the storms by speaking peace over them. It is really wonderful to know that He has power over environmental storms. It is greater still to realize that His peace speaks over our personal and emotional ones too. Hence, living in the peace of God is experiencing His peace when it matters most—in the middle of difficult life circumstances. It is a knowing in our hearts that all is well and that God and life can be trusted, even when everything appears to be falling apart.

I have experienced this abiding peace firsthand, and I can tell you it is real. It has positively been my saving grace during some of the hardest times in my life. During times when I would have expected myself to be falling apart emotionally, instead I felt the supernatural peace and joy of God. This is not to say that I was numb to the pain, either, because I felt that too. The truth is that in God's realm, we can experience pain and peace at the same time. Though this may seem like an absolute contradiction in terms, I assure you, it isn't. As a matter of fact, when we experience peace in pain, we finally understand what Paul was talking about when he referred to God's peace as "the peace that surpasses understanding" (Philippians 4:7 NKJV).

Peace not only provides strength in the midst of our storms, but it also provides supernatural direction for our choices. As previously stated, it is the Holy Spirit that constantly makes this peace available. In fact, the Holy Spirit is everything to the earthbound Christian. He is our guide and our teacher. He is our best friend on this side of eternity. And one of His many roles in our lives is that of providing direction in making decisions that propel our lives forward into the plan of God. The fruit of the Spirit of peace is a key component of this function.

A lot of people call this *intuition,* but it is actually the presence of the Holy Spirit speaking into our spirit. I have come to call this sixth sense within me *peace cues.* Peace cues are internal signals based on the presence or absence of the *feeling* of peace in our hearts. I emphasize the word *feeling* because the Holy Spirit never actually leaves us, therefore neither does His peace. When we experience an absence of peace, it is absent only at the soul level, which pertains to our mind, perceptions, and emotions. When we cannot experience peace at the soul level, it is a powerful indicator that something is not right. For this reason, I have come to rely heavily on peace cues when making decisions.

Life is awesome in that it offers so many opportunities for us to thrive. However, not all opportunities are in our best interest. As human beings, we possess a limited view of the future, often making it difficult to ascertain which course of action to take. That is precisely where the Holy Spirit comes in. Indeed, He always knows what we need and is willing to share it with us, but unless we know how to perceive His wisdom, it cannot truly benefit us. For this reason, learning to perceive the Holy Spirit's abiding direction is one of our many jobs in life.

Thus, paying attention to peace cues is key when confronting a life change or course of action. For example, many times in my own journey, I have been presented with an opportunity that I have felt conflicted about. The opportunity might have seemed amazing at face value, but for some reason unbeknownst to me, I just did not feel peace about it in my heart.

I experienced this powerful direction during a poignant time in my life some years ago, when I was very close to marrying the wrong person (for the second time, mind you). Back then, I was still in the process of learning to listen to peace cues, so all I remember experiencing was a frenzy of uncomfortable emotions—and a lot of fear. After a few weeks, the fear became so intense, I developed asthma symptoms for the very first time. Fortunately, we broke up shortly thereafter. And interestingly enough, when he was gone, so were the fear and the asthma. As uncomfortable as they were, the peace cues in this situation helped me to end a relationship that was not for me. And thank God for that!

At other times in my life, peace cues have worked in the exact opposite manner—they have served to lead my life in a positive direction. For example, when I have been confronted with a good opportunity, I have experienced peace in my heart, a knowing that it is right for me, and an absolute absence of fear. When this occurs, I have learned to move forward in confidence, knowing that God has opened the door and He will orchestrate everything pertaining to it.

Peace cues can also be used to help us make wise decisions pertaining to relationships. When discerning the hearts and intentions of others, they can come in quite handy. A good example is when we have sensed, for some unknown reason, that someone does not have good intentions toward us. Or maybe we had a gut feeling that we should not get involved with a person. We knew it had nothing to do with anything he or she said or did, but it was a *knowing* within us. In these cases, peace cues helped us stay away from harmful individuals.

Peace cues can also reveal someone's character in a positive way. This is evident when we meet someone for the first time, yet we feel instantly connected to that person. We get a good vibe and just know we are meant to team up with that individual in some way. These are both examples of the way God's peace conveys information about people in order to help guide our choices.

Paying attention to peace cues can also be a great tool for navigating relationships effectively. They are helpful when interacting with others by enabling us to act and react in ways that will promote peace and maintain harmony. The author of the Book of Hebrews emphasized that, as God's children, we should always pursue peace in relationships (Hebrews 12:14 NKJV). Sometimes maintaining peace and harmony in relationships is shutting our mouths before offending someone. Other times, it is choosing to be wrong, even when we think we are right. Furthermore, pursuing peace requires that we habitually exercise humility and meekness in our relationships, aspects of God also included in the Holy Spirit package.

Pride, as opposed to humility, cannot stand to be wrong and often chooses to be right in spite of the consequences. When we push in our relationships, we step on people's toes, hurt others' feelings, and offend. When we consistently take this approach, we often find our lives are marked by constant conflict and turmoil. Because everything we do is in the context of relationships, it benefits all of us to learn how to have healthy and happy ones. Thus, paying attention to peace cues and making relationship choices accordingly will make us all-around happier people.

Paying attention to peace cues can also be very useful when conflict does arise in relationships. Here's another example from my own life. Not so long ago, I had angry feelings toward a person in my life who I love very much. I was harboring resentment for a couple of weeks and thinking judgmental thoughts about him. Fortunately, years of abiding in God's peace has made me quite apt at realizing when it is missing from my experience. And in this situation, it was definitely missing.

Negativity, anger, resentment, and the like have this effect on our lives. When we find ourselves in this place, we will be forced to choose between having peace and being angry. The two cannot coexist. In this situation, my anger had caused me to become extremely uncomfortable. And thank God for the discomfort of anger and negativity because it always leads me to do the right thing. Finding my way back to peace once again became my priority, thereby overriding any justification I may have had for staying angry.

I felt I needed to take the first step in making things right. I apologized for my part and expressed my feelings of hurt. We had an adult conversation about the problem, and the issue was resolved. Because I sought harmony in this situation, I was able to release all negative feelings about it; I reunited with my old friend, Peace; and a disagreement that could have lasted a long time was curtailed in minutes. That is the power of peace.

The point is that our insides often tell a story about what is happening outside of us, and it behooves us to listen. I have learned to listen and follow its lead. And in my experience, it has been right 100 percent of the time. Living this way is so much easier than feeling like we have to figure everything out for ourselves—a burden no human being can carry.

It is important for us to realize that the peace of God is not just something that makes us feel good. It is a gift from God that helps us gracefully get through difficult moments in life and know what to do in times of confusion. It conveys a wealth of information about the direction and steps that we should take. And it is there for all of us.

Sadly, many frustrated people struggle to hear God's voice. Learning to discern God's voice does take practice, but it is not rocket science either. Our own intellect is the greatest hindrance when it comes to hearing the voice of God. Other times, people cannot discern the voice of God because of competing voices—the voice of other people telling them what to do; the voice of the devil trying to mislead them; the voice of the world with its misdirected values and ideals; even the voice of their own empty plans and desires.

Learning to discern the voice of God over all others is a skill the Holy Spirit wants to help us all hone in on. As you embark on the journey of learning to listen to and follow God's peace cues, you will learn something remarkable: *you possess all of the answers for life inside of you at all times!* The more you open your heart to this guidance, the more you will find yourself experiencing the peace that surpasses understanding. And once you do, you will become unwilling to live without. You will always find your way back to it as your priorities, actions, and the direction of your life begin to take an effortless turn toward destiny.

Today, choose peace. Let it be the umpire in your life. Choose to listen to its voice within you. It will not mislead you. It will always take you to a good place. It will take you exactly where you *want* to go, even if you do not know it. The peace of God is a gift that has been given to you. Accept it fully today. Live in it. Abide in it. Bask in it. Become addicted to it. Pursue it all the days of your life, for it will lead you in the way everlasting (Psalm 139:24 NKJV).

Lesson 9: Let Peace be the Umpire in Your Life
Questions for Self-reflection

1. What is the difference between the peace the world gives us and the peace that Jesus gives us?

_____

_____

_____

_____

2. Have you experienced times in your life when it felt like the peace of God was absent from your experience? If so, what reasons can you pinpoint for that?

_____

_____

_____

_____

3. What are peace cues?

_____

_____

_____

_____

4. Give two examples of a time in your life when peace cues conveyed information that something or someone was in your best interest, and two examples when they conveyed the opposite?

_____

_____

_____

_____

5. What hinders you from being able to discern the guidance
    of Holy Spirit in your day-to-day life? What would help you
    become more attune to His abiding leadership?

_____

_____

_____

_____

Lesson 10

Trust the Process

I'm like the little girl who had a little curl right in the middle of her forehead. When I was bad, well, I was great at it. I put the "fun" in dysfunctional, as they say. But when my life started changing, much to my surprise, I became very, very good. This reference to the popular poem "There Was a Little Girl" by Henry Wadsworth Longfellow represents how at times we all fall victim to all-or-nothing mentalities. And when these mentalities find their way into our thinking, as it pertains to the process of change and growth, they can be very destructive.

Often, it is as if a light switch goes off in people's minds when they begin to change. The momentum of change and the positive feelings and results associated with it create a deep desire for more. This is good. There is nothing negative about it. What can be detrimental, however, is when we develop perfectionistic attitudes and mindsets toward the process.

Early on, whenever I felt things did not go my way, I too fell victim to this perfectionistic trap. The first few years of my healing journey were riddled with bouts of depression and emotional pain—and not for lack of determination. I wanted so badly to change, and I believed the way to do so was to get involved with as many positive things as I could. Thus, I joined multiple twelve-step groups, attended weekly therapy appointments, went to every conference and seminar available, and faithfully documented every experience in my journal. I was working so hard, so it baffled me as to why I found myself time and time again regressing to old patterns.

I deeply resented the discomfort of the process. I thought it meant that I was doing something wrong as I had not yet learned that life really does begin outside our comfort zone. Discomfort is a necessary part of the process because it means we are pushing up against the status quo. Emotional pain, on the other hand, is largely our own doing. Sadly, it took me years to learn this, thus I struggled all the more.

Before I started my journey, I saw myself as this weak person who could not amount to or overcome anything. Consequently, I mastered the art of denial and other defense mechanisms that assured my conscious mind that all was well in my world. This worked for many years, until the weight of the burden became too much to bear, leading to my nervous breakdown.

When Jesus Christ came into my life, there was no denying it. Everything started changing so rapidly. It was overwhelming—in a good way. I became completely engrossed in all that I was doing and experiencing. I reveled in it and believed it would go on forever. This is the initial part of the change process that twelve-step groups refer to as "being on a pink cloud." The problem with the concept of the pink cloud is that it is expected to end when life and reality hit. To my dismay, this was often my experience. Although I was changing on the inside more and more every day, I did not always see it that way. And such was my dilemma.

The truth is that in the early years, I was still a slave to my emotions. As a result, I was constantly judging myself by what I *felt* at any given moment. When I felt good, all was well. But when I felt lonely, frustrated, or stuck, I became depressed. Invariably, when I became depressed, I would judge myself based on my current state and the things I had yet to accomplish. In those moments, I lost sight of how far I had come and how different my life truly was. I lost sight of the fact that I *was* changing, that I *was* growing, and that I *was* moving forward. In those moments, I lost sight of the fact that *change is a process.*

I thank God for the mirrors I had in my life at that time—all of the individuals who offered love and encouragement and reflected back to me the reality of things. They helped me acknowledge my growth and assisted me in accepting where I was on the journey. They were my teachers in learning the lesson that is central to this chapter—that change is a process.

As a psychotherapist, I have the honor of working with individuals who are also on a journey of change and growth. And often I see them struggling with the same exact thing. They desire to be further ahead. The things they continue to struggle with frustrate them. They resent having to deal with the same old issues time and time again. They become depressed and disheartened with the process. And while I get where they are coming from, I love that today I get to be the mirror in their lives. Today I get to be the person who encourages them to trust and embrace the process.

Indeed, human beings are interesting birds. They are content with laziness and apathy until they are suddenly *not.* They expect to go from dysfunction to self-actualization in sixty seconds flat. Though we tend to look at change based on a time continuum—i.e., we get frustrated when we feel we are not changing fast enough—in actuality, time is not the issue. The real problem arises when people place unrealistic expectations and standards on themselves, others, and the process. They easily become judgmental and critical at the first sign of imperfection or error. Even society teaches, both implicitly and explicitly, that tough love and harsh discipline are the ways to encourage top performance. This, however, could not be further from the truth.

Another thing that people on the journey of change frequently struggle with is going to extremes. Often this is simply part of the process and should be accepted, just as the ups and downs are. It is not uncommon at all that, on the way to finding balance with an issue in our lives, we initially find ourselves doing the exact opposite. Truly, 180 degrees from wrong is still wrong, albeit in the other direction. If we find ourselves experiencing this phenomenon, however, we should fight the urge toward self-judgment and criticism, as these will only create more of its kind.

I struggled with all of these issues until I learned the importance of radical self-acceptance, something I still practice to this day. Self-acceptance is a powerful principle that brings peace in the process and opens doors to change. This famous passage from "The Serenity Prayer" offers amazing wisdom that can be easily applied to the ebbs and flows of change: "God grant me the serenity to accept the things I cannot change, the courage to change the things I can, and the wisdom to know the difference" (Reinhold Niebuhr).

Offering self-acceptance at all times in the journey is absolutely paramount to moving forward and continuing to change. Acceptance does not mean that we give up or surrender to a problem. Acceptance is more an attitude toward the self and life. It is surrendering to God and the process, not the problem. It is trusting that we are progressing, even when we cannot see it. Indeed, the principle of acceptance does not resent change but acknowledges and embraces the process that it is.

In her book *Beyond Codependency*, Melody Beattie depicts this process of change by comparing two arrow-like figures. One arrow is depicted as a straight line shooting upward with no bends or breaks in it. The second is depicted as a line that looks more like a lightning rod, only with the tip of an arrow. It is also shooting upward, but has the backward bends typically seen in illustrations of lightning. She describes that true change is not the arrow shooting upward with no breaks or bends in it, as this is an unrealistic perspective for change. She adds, rather, that the arrow that looks like a lightning rod is the true picture of change, a process that is constantly in flux (1989).

Theoretically speaking, we all wish that change was more like the straight line shooting upward toward perfection. But, like Melody Beattie, I too see change as the arrow that looks like lightning. The backward bends of the lightning rod give the impression that in those moments, one is moving backward. But we also see that after the bend, there is an immediate push upward. In reality, those moments of seeming regression are necessary parts of the process. The fact that we grow uncomfortable with old patterns is evidence that we have, in fact, changed. That discomfort forces us to use our emotional muscles by applying what we have learned along the way.

Furthermore, it is in those challenging moments that we learn to use our coping skills. Thus, we realize that even in the times we were down, great growth and learning were actually taking place, causing us to shoot upward once again in victory. This is the emotional and spiritual equivalent of what happens to our physical muscles when we work them out with weights. The resistance produced by the weight provides the optimal condition for our muscles to increase. Truly, without resistance there would be no growth at all.

Let me give you an example to further accentuate this point. Take an individual who has struggled with depression for many years. One day, she finally gets tired of being sick and tired and becomes determined to change. In that pivotal moment, she develops a fiery determination, causing her to make choices in service to that change.

She starts seeing a therapist and begins to identify thought patterns and triggers to her current state. She also starts reading self-help and spiritual literature, giving her a new perspective on herself and life.

Almost immediately, she starts to feel better and can hardly believe what she is experiencing. Then one day, to her dismay, she wakes up in the morning and notices she is grumpy and negative. She experiences herself feeling more down that she has been in months. She becomes frustrated and fearful that all has been lost. "Have I gone back to my old self?" she wonders in concern.

The truth is, she has not gone back to her old self, nor has she lost the lessons previously gained. The only thing that has happened is that those old patterns, still in the process of being replaced by new ones, continue to exist in her mind. As a result, it is inevitable to experience some form of regression.

Instead of freaking out, she need only understand that change is a process. And included in that process are moments in which she has seemingly moved in a backward direction. Instead of self-judgment, she needs to give herself radical love and acceptance. As she does this and continues on the same path she has been on, she will quickly find herself using the tools she has learned to come out of the funk. Over time, as new behaviors become her new normal, she will notice those moments of regression are fewer and further between.

Each of us goes through this cycle to some degree. And each time we succeed at coming to the other side, we become more resilient. Since on our way to victory we will inevitably experience some failure, resiliency is necessary if we are to fulfill our destinies and live our best lives. In addition, in order to continue on that upward trajectory, we must all learn to move quickly past frustration and into acceptance.

We have all heard the old adage, "Rome wasn't built in a day." When it comes to construction, we get it—buildings do not go up overnight. So why don't we get it when it comes to ourselves? It is important to realize that it is this erroneous perspective that causes so much frustration and not the process itself. This is precisely why acceptance of the process is such a powerful component of change.

As a matter of fact, it was the process itself that taught me the beautiful thing that finally set me free from this unreasonable expectation: I learned that not only was it okay to be wherever I was on the journey, it was the only place I was expected *to* be. In fact, it was the only place I *could* be. Think about it: How could we be anywhere other than where we are? It is a physical impossibility.

More important, I learned that God Himself does not expect me to be anywhere other than where I am. I found out that He understands the process more than I ever could, and that my deep desire to change pleases Him much more than any particular accomplishment. It was in *His* grace, unconditional love, and acceptance that I found the power to accept myself. This allowed me to keep moving forward much more than any amount of harsh discipline or self-judgment could have. Actually, finding that kind of love, support, and acceptance in my heavenly Father enabled me to provide it for myself. And what really rocked my world was finding out that that was the lesson He most wanted me to learn.

Looking back, I realize that I was changing *the things that I could change*—although certainly not perfectly, and definitely not in my time frame. My problem was that I was judging myself nine ways to Sunday every step of the way. In scripture, God is referred to as being *long-suffering*, which is synonymous for *patient*. However, the context of the word *long-suffering* conveys a deeper meaning and the true heart of a loving, gentle God. In fact, *long-suffering* in scripture implies patience, beyond patience, beyond patience, beyond patience, beyond patience, beyond patience. You get the drift. God's patience toward us has no limit and never ends. If we fall a million times, a million times He picks us up, a million times He is there for us, and a million times He whispers in our spirit, "You can do this! I believe in you!"

Furthermore, it is important to note that while setbacks are normal, there are things in us that can actually delay the process for many, many years. Some examples are: impatience toward ourselves, lack of self-acceptance, self-judgment, frustration, condemnation, shame, a feeling that God is mad at or disappointed in us, performance mindset, guilt, unforgiveness, and still others not mentioned. Some of these have been discussed in prior chapters while others were not. Yet they are equally powerful to thwart change.

Basically, any self-defeating or negative belief system or perspective will impede the process. On the other hand, receiving God's love and acceptance, self-love, self-acceptance, obtaining positive attitudes and perspectives, developing patience, and trusting the process will take us deep and far into the journey of change. Beloved, we are in it for the long haul. Life *is* the long haul. Doesn't it make more sense to be kind to ourselves and enjoy the journey along the way?

In addition to the abovementioned hindrances, there is yet another type of belief system that can greatly impede the process. That is when individuals possess erroneous perspectives pertaining to the manner in which change takes place. The human tendency is to attempt to change as much as possible, as quickly as possible. The reality is, however, that permanent change does not happen by taking a few large steps but by taking many small ones, consistently and over time.

I often use an analogy in counseling to help my clients understand how this works: Imagine that I have a leaky faucet in my house. The drip is so minute, though, it seems utterly insignificant. Just one tiny drop at a time ... drip ... drip ... drip ... No biggie, right? Now imagine what would happen if, prior to going to bed, I placed a bucket beneath the drip. In all likelihood, the next morning it would be full and perhaps even overflowing. Suddenly, my perspective regarding the significance of the drip would be drastically different.

Similarly, change seems inconsequential in the moment. It is only when we look at in retrospect that we are able to realize its true impact. One small change after another, after another, after another, and before we know it, we are more different than we ever imagined we could be. Every small change represents a lasting and powerful effect on our ingrained mindsets and patterns of behavior. This inner transformation radiates outward, causing lasting change in our external behaviors. This, and only this, is the true nature of permanent change.

There is one more powerful truth that I would like to share on the topic of change. And it is as profound as it is encouraging. While in the natural sense, the process of change certainly has its ups and downs, I have learned it is not so in the spiritual sense. In the Spirit, we are always moving forward. For this reason, when we are cooperating with the process and in tune with the Spirit of God, we can trust change is taking place beyond our ability to perceive it. At any given moment, there is much more happening that we cannot see than what we can see with our natural eyes.

I remember a poignant moment when I was complaining to God about my struggles on the journey. Admittedly, I did that quite often back then. That day was different, though, because He spoke something to me that forever changed the way I view my experiences. He said, "I am laying a foundation *in* your life that will carry you *through* your life. Will you let Me?" I suddenly understood that God was not as concerned with what I was experiencing as He was about my growth and development. Indeed, God realizes that life is a classroom, and He uses every experience to change belief systems and perspectives in us that conflict with life in the Spirit. This is a process we must all cooperate with if we are to live our potential.

By the same token, dear reader, as you go through its byways and highways, always remember that the path is steeped in grace. Indeed, the beauty of God is that wherever we are, even if we are not ready to cooperate, He is wooing us and preparing our hearts for that state of readiness. Wherever we are on our journey, He is right there with us. But if you are one who is prone to self-judgment, you may be tempted to accuse yourself of not cooperating with God. If that were the case, though, I would encourage you to ask yourself why you would be reading this particular book. After all, only those interested in change would choose to read a book entitled *Life's a Classroom*.

Here's even more amazing news about the journey: There is absolutely no judgment on it—only hope and encouragement. God wants us to change more than we do. And He is willing to stand with us the whole way until we reach His desired end.

So today, relax. Enjoy your day. Enjoy the journey. Embrace the ebbs and flows of change. The process of change itself—and by extension, life—is teaching you the lessons you need, and want, to learn. It is your friend and not your enemy. Today, love yourself. Have patience with yourself. Accept yourself and the process. Today, choose to change the things you can and accept the things you can't. Give up control and surrender to the process. The more you do, the faster you will move through it. So fasten your seat belt, sit back, and enjoy the ride. And by all means, do whatever you want with your hands and feet. It's your ride. It's your journey. Live it fully!

Lesson 10: Trust the Process
Questions for Self-reflection

1. Think about your journey with God. What have the ups and downs of the process taught you so far?

_____

_____

_____

_____

2. I listed some hindrances to change in this chapter. Which ones in particular have hindered change in your journey?

_____

_____

_____

_____

3. What does the *Serenity Prayer* say we should do about the things we currently cannot change? Have you resisted doing that in the past and why?

_____

_____

_____

_____

4. Name the things in your life that you *can* change right now? For each one, list some action steps that will bring about that change.

_____

_____

_____

_____

5. Why is self-love and self-acceptance so important when it comes to the process of change?

_____

_____

_____

_____

References

Alcoholics anonymous (fourth edition). (2001). New York, NY: Alcoholics Anonymous World Services Inc.

Amplified Bible (classic edition). (1987). Grand Rapids, MI: Zondervan Publishing House.

Amplified Bible (expanded edition). (1987). Grand Rapids, MI: Zondervan Publishing House.

Beattie, M. (1989). *Beyond codependency: And getting better all the time.* Center City, MN: Hazelden.

Character. (n.d.). In *Merriam-Webster's Online Dictionary.* Retrieved November 30, 2015, from http://merriam-webster.com/dictionary/character

Evolve. (n.d.). In *Merriam-Webster's Online Dictionary.* Retrieved October 15, 2015, from http://merriam-webster.com/dictionary/evolve

Gilbert, M. (2006). *Eat, Pray, Love.* New York, NY: Penguin.

Nelson's NKJV study Bible, new king james version. (1997). Nashville, TN: Thomas Nelson Inc.

Peace. (n.d.). In *Merriam-Webster's Online Dictionary*. Retrieved December 28, 2015, from http://www.merriam-webster.com/dictionary/peace

Pessimism. (n.d.). In *Merriam-Webster's Online Dictionary*. Retrieved November 5, 2015, from http://merriam-webster.com/dictionary/pessimism

Precede. (n.d.). In *Merriam-Webster's Online Dictionary*. Retrieved November 30, 2015, from http://merriam-webster.com/dictionary/precede

Sanders, M. and Sillers, T. (2000). I hope you dance [Recorded by Lee Ann Womack and Sons of the Dessert]. On *I hope you dance* [CD]. Nashville, TN: MCA Nashville.

Shakespeare, W. (1992). *Hamlet*. Mowat, B. and Werstine, P. (eds.). New York, NY: Simon & Schuster Paperbacks.

Zeitgeist. (n.d.). In *Wikipedia*. Retrieved November 1, 2015, from http://en.wikipedia.org/wiki/Zeitgeist

Printed in the United States
By Bookmasters